For Wally

I am thankful for your patience and for
supporting me to tell my story.

I LOVE YOU!

In Memoriam
Morena

For Ann & Bernie

Live your best life,

For Ann & Bernie

Live your best life,

Contents

Introduction

Moments. All the moments we have in our lives have gotten us to where we stand today. Moments shape and mold our lives—some happy, others sad, some so big they alter our course for better or worse, and others so insignificant that they fade into lost memories. Many of these moments are within our sphere of influence and other moments are far beyond the reach of our control. Some of my best moments are when I met Wally Brewster—the man who would become the U.S. ambassador to the Dominican Republic—and when same-sex marriage became legal in the United States, allowing Wally to become my husband.

I've had many other remarkable and memorable moments for which I am grateful. I have met presidents, prime ministers, dignitaries, aristocrats, celebrities, people of influence in the private and public sector, as well as those with no fame or public notoriety whatsoever. All of these people have touched my life with friendship, kindness, and love. I've had experiences beyond my wildest imagination. Experiences like this don't often happen to a guy like me, a poor kid from a small town in eastern Oklahoma. But they did—and this is my book of moments.

I remember the moment I fell in love with politics and public service. I was playing in a school tennis tournament in McAlester, Oklahoma, in fall 1978. I was 14 years old. McAlester is a mid-sized town about 40 minutes' drive from my hometown Henryetta. The Department of Corrections had its largest prison there, which housed the most notorious murderers and death row inmates in the state. It seemed nobody could mention the town of McAlester without mentioning the state prison.

McAlester was also the home of the former Speaker of the U.S. House of Representatives Carl Albert. He served as the Speaker during the Watergate scandal and President Richard Nixon's resignation from office. Our fellow Oklahoman was a significant player in one of the most tumultuous political investigations in American history. I listened to many conversations about politics from adults and was exposed to the importance of political leadership in my school. It seemed so interesting to me, a way to change the trajectory of things to come.

On the day of my tennis tournament, David Boren, then governor of Oklahoma, was campaigning in McAlester for U.S. Senate. He approached our teams and chaperones and spoke with the adults among us. Then he took time to meet the players and wished us luck in the tournament. That made a huge impression on me—no doubt at that point in my life the governor was the highest-ranking elected official I had ever met.

In my junior high civics class, I had learned what the government was and how it affected people's lives. I was far too young to distinguish the difference between Republicans and Democrats or what party affiliation meant, but the few people I knew who identified politically were Democrats and they seemed to be good people to me. After I met Governor Boren, I found out he was a Democrat and I thought he must be a very good person because of his gesture of kindness to us kids at the tennis tournament. I decided I was going to support Governor Boren's campaign to win the U.S. Senate seat from Oklahoma, even though I wasn't nearly old enough to vote.

The extent of my campaign experience at the ripe old age of 14 was wearing a "Boren for Senate" t-shirt and handing out flyers in our hometown Labor Day Parade. Nonetheless, I felt like I was participating in the democratic process. I had been bitten by the political bug and it influenced me and stoked my passion for democracy to this day.

I believe we all have an obligation to serve our democracy, to serve our fellow man, and to create a better world for future generations. I believe most Americans fulfill this obligation in various ways, including charitable giving, volunteering, and voting. I also believe most Americans hold themselves accountable to the privilege of being American. I had the opportunity to observe leadership up close and personal and learned early in my life what it meant to "serve." I am sure the fact that Governor Boren won the election and became the U.S. senator from Oklahoma helped mold my impression.

There were the far-too-many moments in my childhood when I was among the victimized: when I was humiliated in front of my whole high school, reminiscent of the movie *Carrie*, minus the blood...when my car was vandalized by a classmate...when I was ashamed of where I lived and afraid of who I was...and sadly so many more experiences from my youth that put me in survival mode. These moments steeled my resolve to always be a champion for the underdog and those without a voice. They grew my determination to make something of myself and speak up for those who couldn't. I was a scrawny little kid in no position to fight back. I had a dysfunctional home life that could be peaceful or filled with drama at any given moment. My experiences helped me realize the world was not a nice place for poor people like me. Despite the fact I had no control over the financial well-being of my family, I still suffered the consequences through no action of my own. I was 16 years old when I came to the realization life is just not fair, especially when you're poor.

Looking back, I don't blame or harbor resentment toward those kids who bullied and abused me, or even the adults who enabled it. I would never recommend my experiences as a form of character building, but the lessons I learned helped me create an iron will to succeed, without which I wouldn't be where I am today.

The other huge lesson I take from my experiences in my adolescence, in my travels, and from living in the Dominican Republic is that not all poor people are bad people, not all rich people are good people, and not all people who go to church and call themselves Christians are actually people of God. I developed my sense of activism for the marginalized because I was one of them. I remember when we were serving in the Dominican Republic being told by our security team that there were certain areas of the city we just were not allowed to go. I finally figured out that, yes, those areas were filled with crime, but the main reason was they were filled with the poor.

Despite some of my allies who would rather me not say anything, I needed to be public in my efforts to help these people, and many others like them. Not for any personal gain or notoriety, but because for far too long minorities and marginalized people have been told to be quiet. I was told to be quiet for most of my life but once I actually found my voice, I wasn't going to waste it by accommodating the wishes of others. So it should come as no surprise that I believe passionately in helping poor and marginalized people better their stations. Anything I can do to help others out of the same situation I grew up in makes my own challenges worth the suffering. And that is why I will always, as long as there is air in my lungs, fight for those who can't fight for themselves.

I've had moments in my professional life where I spoke my mind with honesty and transparency. I knew in reality I was not speaking for me, I was speaking for communities that would never be invited or given a public platform in which to express themselves, like when I participated in a flight attendants' strike. And becoming a respected professional grew my capacity to be an influencer for the causes for which I fought. During my real estate career in Chicago I served on the board of an organization whose primary purpose was to serve public school at-risk youth in the city, youth that lacked a stable home life, or in some cases even a home. With the support of BUILD, we were able to provide a structure that gave these kids an opportunity that otherwise would have been impossible for them to experience.

I had moments when I began my real estate business in Chicago where I did everything I could to engage with and work with people in the business who needed a helping hand. I hired people I didn't need and I supported organizations I couldn't afford to help because my youthful experiences taught me karma is real and when someone opens a door for you, the last thing you do is slam it shut in the face of the person behind you.

Then there are all the moments I felt loved. I finally realized my parents loved me when they came to our wedding and to Wally's swearing-in. I never felt unloved or uncared for, but despite a roof over my head and food on our table, I always felt alone. My family was not overly demonstrative; we did not tell each other "I love you." That was something very foreign to me. I knew in my soul my parents loved me, because who, but a loving parent, would agree to a guardianship change for their child's own mental health and well-being? But I never felt it in my heart.

I am glad that part of me matured, and that I can now accept the love they have for me without judgment despite their way of professing it to me. I have learned to tell my family and friends that I love them, and I am not afraid to hug them. If someone doesn't return that love, mine is still just as genuine. That kind of trust in myself took a long time to come to terms with, primarily because of my paranoia of being rejected. But that paranoia no longer exists; my emotional self has grown. Love is something Dominican people taught me so much about. There is something about how love in the Latino culture is expressed—openly and beautifully among family, friends, and even perfect strangers— that is bigger than the culture itself.

There were the moments when Wally and I were living in the Dominican Republic during his ambassadorship where I saw true friendships blossom. I connected with a few people who genuinely reached out and validated me as a person. These are the people who extended invitations to me, not because I lived with the ambassador or for what they could get out of me, but because they were interested in knowing who I was and what I brought to the table. I did not expect to be treated equally from such people of influence. I appreciated their invitations to breakfast where we would talk about policy and the future of the relationship between our countries, and their invitations to the local tavern for a beer for the sole reason just to get to know me better. There were a few couples who always invited me to private family dinners at their homes because they were actually interested in the causes I championed. I hope they know how much it meant to me that their gestures were sincere and genuine. I will always cherish those moments.

Sharing my moments provides context as to how I navigated the turbulent waters of being a diplomatic spouse. Many protocols exist for diplomats, but there are no guidebooks or formal support measures on how to be the spouse of someone serving the United States abroad. Spouses are expected to serve alongside their diplomatic husbands and wives—but how? I had to forge my own path, as all spouses do, and depend on my own personal experiences to maneuver many situations. I faced additional challenges as a diplomatic spouse because I am gay, and I braved each new one with creativity, a positive spirit, and an eye toward building a better tomorrow. At times, that required me to break traditional protocols.

A spouse's role goes far beyond being a companion at diplomatic events. I went to the Dominican Republic with an eye toward helping marginalized people. Despite set protocols of where I should or shouldn't go, I went to the *bateys* in the Dominican Republic to offer goodwill and kindness to the poor people who lived there. I worked alongside humanitarian aid workers to support their efforts in alleviating poverty and the stress that people living in poverty endure. I openly advocated for various humanitarian aid issues, including child pregnancy, public health, justice initiatives, gender-based violence, and LGBT issues.

As a political spouse in the public eye, my actions and reactions were examined and judged by the court of public opinion. So I took the high road when Cardinal Nicolás de Jesús López Rodríguez slandered my husband by calling him a faggot in a public televised speech and when he continued to spew hatred at us throughout our tenure in the Dominican Republic. I had been called a faggot since third grade, so a little name-calling wasn't going to adversely affect my experience as a representative of President Barack Obama. The cardinal's vulgar displays of bigotry, racism, and homophobia served to show the world that he was no embodiment of the morality he espoused; they only exposed him as a small-minded, hypocritical fanatic whose time in power was running out. I stood strong and proud, and despite their actions, the cardinal and other evangelical leaders in the Dominican Republic in no way adversely affected my image of the Church or any religion. I stood on my faith, and continued to believe in God. To this day, I openly support an individual's right to practice religion and pray to God, regardless of whether it aligns with my own beliefs or not and regardless of who leads the institution.

I share my story because, despite my austere childhood, a person like me—or you—can accomplish the unimaginable and thrive in the face of hatred, or despair, or insurmountable odds. Haters do nothing but disseminate noise and we all have enough noise in our lives. I hope my story can inspire you to live far beyond the limitations other people place on you. I don't claim to be perfect, for I know that I am not, and I continue to make mistakes and choices that leave me wanting a do-over. But forward is really the only action that will lead us to happiness. I want to plant seeds of resiliency and model behavior that will help you overcome obstacles.

This is the story of my truth as I know it and I have no doubt there will be a few who will respond with noise. I do not want to leave you the impression that I am speaking for anyone other than me. There are many diplomatic spouses whose experiences have varied greatly from mine, there are many school children who will never experience being bullied or teased, and there are many in our nation's population who never had to wait for the Supreme Court to validate their equality. But these are my moments—the good ones and some I wish had never happened—that contributed to who I am today, a man who speaks out and embraces life. I want you to join me in living big and speaking loudly.

Part I

1: Small Town Oklahoma

Henryetta, Oklahoma, 1970s

My life did not begin in a way that would lead you to suspect I would have such extraordinary experiences as an adult. After moving from California to Oklahoma City, our family settled in Henryetta, Oklahoma, where I spent my adolescent years from fourth grade through tenth grade. Growing up poor in this small, rural, eastern Oklahoma town wasn't the most nurturing place for a young gay man like me. These were not good times, and reflecting on my childhood I can't recall one really good memory of my time in Henryetta. Even today, I rarely return because of the pain that resurfaces every time I go there. When my family first moved to Henryetta, we lived on 14th Street, not far from the city's Main Street tennis courts and a block from the neighborhood market Kern's Korner, gas station, and liquor store.

Saved by Tennis

I spent a lot of time watching kids play tennis at the courts on Main Street, just a few blocks from our house. Henryetta had a vibrant tennis program primarily due to Dr. Carl Smith, who I was told funded the program for the town. But tennis was a rich kid's sport, and my family was the opposite of rich. One needed proper tennis shoes, sportswear, and a tennis racket. My family was in no position to afford any of these things, so I watched from the sidelines as others played.

I begged my mom for a tennis racket, and eventually she bought me one at a local five and dime, the small market that carried items like records, clothes, housewares, and other odds and ends. The rackets weren't really proper ones, they were really children's toys. That was all we could afford, and I had to make do with it or go without. It cost $5, which to my family was an extraordinary amount of money to spend on a toy.

I would take my racket and hit the ball against the concrete wall at the far end of the courts. I would spend hours and hours with a ball and that racket, just hitting the ball against the concrete wall. One day while I played alone, an older kid from high school asked if he could borrow my racket to play tennis with his friends. I was in the sixth grade and wasn't really sure if I should allow some big kid I didn't know to take my racket, so I said I couldn't let him use it. He offered to buy it from me, and I said my mom gave it to me, so I couldn't sell it to him. He then offered me $10. Now I wasn't a brilliant kid, but I was smart enough to know that if I sold him the racket for $10 and then bought another racket for $5, I would have $5 left! So, I sold him the racket for $10 and proudly went home to tell my mom.

Unfortunately, she was not as proud of me as I was of myself. She got very upset with me because I didn't understand the sacrifice she had to make to spend $5 on something she really couldn't afford. She emphasized that I needed to learn to appreciate the sacrifice she had made for me. I eventually bought another racket and don't even remember what I spent the remaining $5 on, but I guiltily learned to never again profit from my mother's generosity.

During the summers, the high school tennis coach would give free tennis lessons to kids who signed up at the Main Street courts. I took advantage of these free tennis lessons. By this time, I had become pretty good at controlling the ball because I had spent so much time hitting it against that concrete wall, but I had no real understanding of the game or the other skills it involved. During these lessons, I learned those other skills pretty quickly, and by the time I reached seventh grade, I tried out and made it onto the junior high tennis team.

I had also become best friends with John Kern, whose family owned Kern's Korner, the local market close to my house. He also played tennis. If not for John, I would never have developed my tennis game because he and a girl named Joy were the only two people who would actually play with me. The rest of the kids refused to play against me and tormented and bullied me when I would play. It's a wonder why I continued to play at all.

My bullies didn't know that no amount of tormenting from them could compare to the possible hostile environment I might face at home.

Life at Home

My father was a severe alcoholic and honestly a mean drunk. I have no doubt it is painful for my father to read these words; however, it's my truth and it plays a key role to understanding my journey. It is painful for me to write about my father in this way. I am thankful those days are behind me, and him, but the memories live with me daily. Those memories push me to do better, to work harder, and to understand that not all bad situations result in a bad outcome in the future.

My parents had married young and had four kids by the time they were 30 years old with no real means to support us. My dad never had a formal education, but he did work hard as an auto body repairman and painter, fixing wrecked cars. But hard work doesn't always equal high rewards. This was very laborious work and not a pleasant environment to work in, but that was his way of making money.

We lived in a small two-bedroom house that my paternal grandmother had owned, which was on the side of a hill next to a creek. This house had electricity but didn't have central heat or air conditioning. In the small living room was an open-flame gas heater used to heat the entire house, and when it got really cold my mom would turn on the gas stove in the kitchen to provide extra heat. In the summer we had a water cooler that blew air through the living room window and we would place box fans in the bedroom windows to draw the cool air from the water cooler through the house.

My three sisters shared one of the bedrooms and my parents the other; I slept on the living room sofa. By the time I was in sixth grade, I really began to realize how poor we were. I remember wanting to have a birthday party. My mom insisted that if I wanted to invite my friends from school then I had to do it at our little house on the side of the hill. I was very hesitant because I didn't want what few friends I had to see where I lived. I was already being verbally and physically bullied at school, and I didn't want to risk losing the few friends I had by allowing them to see our house. Also, I never knew when my dad would show up completely intoxicated and cause a scene.

I had the party, anyway. I remember my friend Laura's reaction when her mom drove her up to the house and she looked at me and asked, "This is where you live?" in a surprised and hesitant voice. I was mortified. Despite my anxiety, I had fun. My mom came up with some games we played, and we had cake and ice cream. That was the only time I invited friends to my house until we moved to a new house when I was in ninth grade.

Despite all the family drama during my childhood and the verbal and physical abuse I suffered in school, I earned decent grades and developed a competitive tennis game good enough to make the high school team. By the time I was in ninth grade, one of my sisters had dropped out of high school and had her first child, and my other two sisters had graduated high school and moved out of the house. My parents and I moved to a new three-bedroom, two-bathroom, brick house on the outskirts of town. I was so proud of my parents and for the first time thought things might actually be looking up for us.

I also got a part-time job working at a Sonic Drive-In and bought a car between my freshman and sophomore years. It was a beautiful used midnight blue 1977 Chevrolet Camaro. All seemed to be looking up... until I was reminded by a supposed friend that the home my parents bought was an Indian home paid for by the Cherokee Nation—basically a welfare house—and that only poor kids worked during high school.

I remember this clearly because it came from someone I really thought was my friend. The truth was the house was financed originally by a low-income loan guaranteed by the tribal community, but my parents had to work and make mortgage payments just like anyone else who bought a house. My mom always said that a person who likes you because of your financial position, rich or poor, is not a friend at all. My mom was right, but her words offered little comfort to me as an adolescent seeking affirmation from my peers.

Socially, I was in no better place than I had ever been despite my parents' efforts to provide us with a better home and despite my own initiative to work and pay for a car I really couldn't afford. After entering tenth grade, things went from bad to worse as the bullying and physical abuse escalated. My grades began to suffer drastically.

That year my car was vandalized by a female classmate who was the friend of one of my close friends. This girl keyed my car—she literally scratched the paint down the side of my car with a key—during a high school football game. When the game was over, a small group of kids conveniently stood around my car to witness my reaction. My friend ultimately told me who had vandalized my car but refused to admit it publicly, because she didn't want to get her friend in trouble. That ended our friendship. I again reflected on my mother's words: a person who likes you because of your financial position, rich or poor, is no friend at all.

As that summer passed, I continued to work at the Sonic Drive-In. It was a good summer. My mom had become part owner and full-time manager of the Sonic. We would close the drive-in, make the night deposit at the bank, and then go to Love's Country Store to buy honey buns to take home to heat in our new microwave. We would drink coffee and eat our treats, talking until late into the night. That particular summer is one of the only times I remember ever being happy in Henryetta.

Getting "Elected"

As I entered my eleventh-grade year of high school, it didn't take long for all my happiness to go to hell. Coming off a good summer working with my mom and saving a little money to pay for my car insurance and gas, I was excited about my last two years of high school. Our tennis team was positioned to do very well both my junior and senior years; in fact, we were predicted to win the state championship both years. I only had one friend on the team, and despite the efforts of the rest of the team to bully me, I remained a solid member of the team and even improved my game. I had a lot of hope and promise that my life would begin to improve.

Within the first few weeks of my junior year, the school conducted its all-school orientation assembly where all tenth, eleventh, and twelfth graders gathered in the auditorium for a review of school policy, announcements of special activities, and, as those in the South do, to shine the light on that year's high school varsity football team. There were fewer than 300 kids in the entire high school—everyone knew everyone and we all attended classes in the same building. The need for orientation was non-existent; the assembly was more of a way to promote certain school activities, namely football. After all, in the South nothing else matters except high school varsity football. The assembly also spotlighted the varsity cheerleaders, and held elections for the officers of the pep club.

The pep club was a girls' organization, a southern cheer squad of wannabe cheerleaders supporting and worshiping the varsity football team by waving pom-poms and wearing matching t-shirts. The officers of the pep club were elected by the entire school at the assembly, but that really meant the rest of us sat around while the football players and cheerleaders nominated the officers by level of popularity. I was in the high school band and attended all the high school football games. I was close friends with some of the varsity cheerleaders and was more than happy to drive them around town or run errands for them so they would continue to be my friend. Unbeknownst to me, the football team and varsity cheerleaders had hatched a plan to humiliate me.

When the officer nomination process started, the first person to stand was a football player who nominated me as president! The entire assembly laughed uproariously. I was completely humiliated. I told the teacher leading the assembly I had no interest in being pep club president, but he told me every nominee must be put forth to a vote. So, there I sat being humiliated by the entire school while this ass of a teacher played along.

Ever since my eighth-grade civics class, I had a keen interest in politics and government. I aspired to become elected to public office one day ever since I handed out campaign flyers for Governor Boren's U.S. Senate campaign in 1978. Actually, I had dreams of being the governor of Oklahoma. Boren won the election and the pride I felt at being a small part of his campaign made me feel part of a greater community and part of a much broader effort to help those in need. So in my mind I, too, would run for governor one day or maybe even senator!

I learned from the pep club nomination experience that there were very ugly sides to being elected to a public office by a community of your peers. As students returned to class following the assembly, I went to my car and drove home, feeling miserable, dejected, humiliated, and angry.

My mom wasn't home, but it didn't take long in our small town for her to find out I was. She called to ask why I was home, and I told her I quit school. She immediately began screaming at me, telling me that if she had to sit in my classroom every day to ensure I finished school then by God I was going to finish high school. Even in those days I could be pretty determined, and after about a week of refusing to leave the house, I think my parents both realized I was not returning to school.

I offered a solution: let me live with my cousin about 90 miles away in Tecumseh and finish high school there. After a discussion with my aunt and uncle, they agreed. So, the next week I left to live with them. I enrolled in the new school and got a job at the local supermarket to pay for my gas and car insurance, and to give my aunt and uncle a few dollars for the inconvenience of my being there.

My cousin was a very good basketball player and was in the ninth grade at the time, two years younger than me. He made the varsity high school basketball team as a freshman; he was good looking and extremely popular. This was awesome for me as I became instantly popular because of him. This school experience was life changing for me.

Family Dynamics

Both my parents as well as my aunt and uncle thought I would return to my parents' house after a few weeks. My aunt and uncle were not well-off people, and my uncle drank as much as my dad did. The agreement was that I would pay them to stay in their home. They rarely had food in the house, and my uncle drank a lot and often fought with my aunt, much like my parents. Because the grocery store I worked at allowed employees a 50 percent discount, I decided to buy groceries for the house as well as snacks, sodas, and treats I never had as a kid.

I assumed my aunt and uncle would be very happy since I was able to take what little money I would give them out of my paycheck and double it in value with food for the family. I was wrong. I overheard them fighting about me and the fact I assumed they couldn't afford groceries for their kids. My misguided effort at kindness had actually offended them. They had been counting on the money in exchange for me staying there and now I couldn't afford to pay them. My parents called the next morning, and asked me to visit them in Henryetta. When I arrived, they informed me I couldn't return to my aunt and uncle's house—they told me I had to move home. What I remember most is trying to make my parents realize if I couldn't stay at the new school then that was the end of my life. And I meant it literally.

I had contemplated suicide multiple times as a teenager. I knew that being gay was not a life that would allow me to accomplish the things I dreamed about, like being elected to public office. I would never be the boss at a company because I would be fired the minute someone found out who I really was. I would never have a family that I could come home to and build a life with because it was against the law. Men were not allowed to live together in towns like where I grew up. How would I ever have enough money to live in a big city? So I thought about killing myself, but there were two reasons I never attempted suicide: I never had the courage—I was afraid and it scared me to die—and the church said it was wrong and I would burn in hell. I never believed I would burn in hell for being gay but I believed that I would if I killed myself. So I chose to live my living hell instead.

I clung to a small spark of hope. My dad had a younger sister who also lived in Tecumseh. She was a single mom with two young girls. She lived in a small place and could barely support herself, but miraculously she agreed I could stay with her. I never made the grocery mistake again. I paid her out of my paychecks the agreed amount and did a lot of babysitting.

This new living situation wasn't entirely smooth. I wanted to play tennis at my new school and word had traveled that I was a competitive tennis player, so the high school tennis coach was very keen on me being at his school and joining his tennis team. In order to play high school sports, you had to live with your parents or legal guardian in the school district where you were attending school. I recall the policy having something to do with not having ringers play for other school's team. Sports, football in particular, are everything in these rural towns, so I wouldn't be surprised today if that were still actually the case. I wasn't living with my parents or a legal guardian, and my parents had no ability or intention to move to Tecumseh so I could play tennis there. In my mind, there was only one thing to do—allow my aunt to become my legal guardian. I was young and had no idea what that really meant, I just wanted to play tennis. I don't have any idea how the conversation went between my aunt and my parents, but they acquiesced and allowed my legal guardianship to be changed. We even had to go before a judge at the county courthouse. I remember being very nervous and afraid, but I was more afraid of returning to Henryetta.

I see now that it must have been a very difficult decision for my parents, particularly my mother. I am not a parent, but I fully understand giving up legal guardianship of her child must have been gut-wrenching for her. My guardianship's legal status never changed a single thing as it related to my relationship with my parents or my aunt, but it is still something I can't ever imagine doing if I had a child. But my life had been beyond miserable until that point, and for all practical purposes I was going to destroy my life if an agreement could not be reached. I would have dropped out of school, gotten a job making minimum wage, and followed wherever life's path was to lead me. There is nothing wrong with working for minimum wage—most of our country does—but you never get to be the decision maker when you're working in entry-level positions your entire life. Without a high school diploma, that probably would have been my only option. I didn't mind working minimum wage jobs then—they built great character in me and exposed me to many realities of life that I still benefit from today—but I did want to be the decision maker one day.

I am ever-grateful to my parents and my aunt for the great sacrifice they made so I could have a brighter future. I applied myself in school and took as many elective classes as possible. I graduated high school early in December of my senior year.

Looking Back, Looking Forward

With hindsight giving me perfect vision—despite looking back with emotion regarding my experiences—I do not harbor hostility toward those who bullied me. I learned that young people have the ability to ascertain a person's character but not necessarily make the best decisions regarding what's good and bad because they are influenced and reinforced by their peers, parents, or other influential individuals in their life. Generally speaking, most young people are just seeking social acceptance and popularity. I believe we are all born pure and without sin (a theology I have long been in conflict with my church). I do believe we are exposed to sin extremely early in life, but more so we learn from and are influenced by the sway of others. As babies and toddlers we live in a world of curiosity and learning. We grow and our love for humanity matures but unfortunately as we grow up, environmentally we are exposed to many of life's negatives such as hypocrisy, anger, and meanness either by family, friends, or community. When this happens, we are too young to differentiate influence from reality and our hostility is born. As we grow, we learn from our environment how to act accordingly based on community or family norms, be they good or bad. We are taught that people different from us are bad, that victory is success, that power is the ultimate influencer. I wasn't picked on, teased, and ultimately abused by my peers because they were inherently bad people; they bullied me because they were taught by someone who influenced them that that kind of behavior was acceptable and that the feelings of the people they bullied didn't matter.

My life completely changed when I started college at the University of Oklahoma. I loved college, despite working 40 hours a week between waiting tables and work-study programs to pay for my living expenses. I got Pell Grants, low-income-student loans, and a few minor scholarships for minority students to help me string together tuition. I didn't make the best grades and I didn't graduate summa cum laude, but I was the first person of my extraordinarily large family ever to go to or graduate from a four-year college.

My early experiences and influences with politics launched my desire to participate in government. While at the University of Oklahoma, I participated in all sorts of governmental activities. Although I ultimately graduated with a business degree, my passion always was political education. During the summer break of my senior year in college, I worked for U.S. Congressman James R. Jones from Tulsa, and ultimately worked on his U.S. Senate campaign. He lost the election but went on to serve as the U.S. ambassador to Mexico for President Bill Clinton, which piqued my interest in foreign policy and clearly influenced my continued participation in the political arena.

During this time in my life, there were a few people who opened doors for me and extended not just emotional support but financial generosity as well. Most of those experiences were when I was seeking employment in college. After my first semester in college, I ran out of money. Betty, the owner of the merchant's association in Ada, Oklahoma, gave me a chance and I have no doubt her business partner Bonnie had great influence in that opportunity. I wasn't afraid of hard work and I was a quick study, but I honestly didn't have a clue what I was doing. These perfect strangers took a gamble on this unprepared kid, gave me a chance and opportunity, and under their wings, I gained confidence and learned gratitude and the art of paying it forward.

When I was young, I always knew there were shadows of aspiration inside me. But it took me years to learn who I was, to figure out where

I wanted to go, what I wanted out of life, and how to get there. I will never look back and think, "Wow, those kids did me a favor because they made my life a living hell," but I do reflect on my experiences knowing they made me a better man. As I grew up, I thankfully developed enough self-awareness to stand on my own truth. I struggled to find my own voice, but when I finally did, I was committed to never allowing it to be silent again.

2: New Adventures

I wasn't actively seeking a relationship when I was living in Dallas in 1989, so meeting my future husband was the pretty much furthest thing from my mind. I was working for American Airlines as an international flight attendant. I loved my life—most of it, anyway—my job, and the friends I made in and around the airline industry. Dallas seemed to me to be a major city, but it was actually rather small by today's standards. Communities and cultures in the late 1980s/early 1990s were somewhat insular and the gay community, as it was called then, was isolated in the safe haven of the Oak Lawn neighborhood adjacent to Highland Park, one of the wealthiest zip codes in the country.

Early that year I moved to the west side of Oak Lawn with a friend of mine from college who was also working for American Airlines. Like me, he had recently "come out of the closet" and embraced his own sexuality as a gay man. It was comforting to have a friend by my side as I explored this new life. My work hours were inconsistent and that made it difficult to pursue other friendships outside the industry. The typical 40-hour full-timer and members of the business community didn't really understand our vocational choice. To them, I was nothing more than a waiter in the sky. Nonetheless life was great because I was, for the first time in my life, comfortable with who I was and was in an industry where being transparent about my personal life wouldn't get me fired.

I excelled at American Airlines, personally and professionally. Personally, I made many friends within the industry. I worked out of the airline headquarters in Dallas/Fort Worth. It was a popular place to be based because it was a very economical place to live for a flight attendant like me who didn't make a lot of money. This also meant that the base was filled with some of the most senior flight attendants in the system. Seniority is paramount in the airline industry. Experienced and senior flight attendants selected their schedules first and the junior staff got the leftovers. In 1989 when I arranged a transfer to the DFW international base, I was the youngest and most junior non-foreign-language speaking flight attendant at the base by a long shot. I found myself flying trips to Europe and Japan with women who were my grandmother's age. They were wonderful and extremely kind to me and I learned a great deal of life's lessons from them.

Professionally, I made a lot of mistakes because I was in my early 20s and had not had a lot of life experience. But with each mistake I made and each experience I encountered, I did my best to learn and apply the lessons to living a more productive life. Despite my youth and inexperience, I worked hard and developed a great deal of notoriety among my co-workers. I was recognized by my peers and my supervisors as a dedicated and hardworking employee, and was nominated for American Airlines' annual Professional Flight Attendant Award (PFA). Nationwide, awards ceremonies were held at the different locations where the airline had offices; depending where you were based, the ceremony would vary.

I was very excited, in part because of the honor, and in part because I had a friend based in New York who had also been nominated for the award. His PFA ceremony was held in New York at Tavern on the Green in Central Park about three months before the DFW ceremony, and he told me about the grand evening of dinner and dancing. I had a problem, though. I didn't own a proper suit because I had never had an occasion where I needed one and really, I couldn't afford one. My roommate had been to Boston on a layover and told me about the store Filene's Basement, where you could buy designer clothing at a steep discount. As airline employees we were able to fly standby—first class, too, but those days are long gone!—so we flew to Boston to check out Filene's Basement. It was everything that my friend claimed it to be and I purchased a handsome suit to wear to my pending PFA award ceremony.

Here is where my expectations and my reality collided. Unlike the magical evening my New York friend attended, the PFA ceremony in Dallas was held on a Thursday afternoon at the Hotel Crescent Court near downtown—one of Dallas's finest properties—and fell far short of what I had anticipated. Lunch and the entertainment of a fashion show awaited me. The designer was Victor Costa, a knock-off ball gown designer who was very famous in the north Texas social community, but contrary to stereotypes, peaked no interest in this 25-year-old gay man. The ceremony ended following lunch about 1:00 p.m., and the strongest liquid served was iced tea.

Life's Random Moments

All dressed up with no place to go, I stopped for a drink on my way home. I headed through the Oak Lawn neighborhood, where practically all the gay bars in Dallas were located on one street. The most popular bar was JR's Bar & Grille, named after J.R. Ewing, the main character from the 1980s television show *Dallas*. It's sister bar where gay women gathered was named Sue Ellen's, after J.R. Ewing's wife of course. I didn't have an office to return to, so I used the pay phone—no cell phones or internet then!—to leave a message for my roommate to join me at JR's. While I was waiting for my roommate to arrive I was the solo customer at the bar. JR's resembled any other tavern on any other street in the United States. It is located on the busy corner of Cedar Springs and Throckmorton, fronted by large plate glass windows perfect for people watching. The bar was a traditional oak bar with barstools lining the sides and neon beer signs placed throughout the pub. It smelled of a mix of beer, alcohol, and cigarettes. Remember, this was also long before people stopped smoking in public places.

I didn't pay much attention at first to Wally, the handsome young man who had walked into the bar that Thursday afternoon. I assumed he was either meeting a friend or going to use the restroom. Shortly, he returned to the front of the bar where I was sitting and started a conversation with me. He was extremely nice and had been having lunch at a restaurant across the street with some friends. He was on vacation, so he didn't have to go back to work. We chatted at bit, exchanged phone numbers, and he left. He certainly left an impression on me because I called him later that day and left a message. He called me back and we arranged to meet for a Saturday brunch at Luckys Café on Oak Lawn. Luckys was well known for having a large gay clientele and was a comfortable place for two men to have brunch together without harboring strange looks.

That is how it all began and 30 years later, having encountered a few bumps in the road, navigated a few pot holes, and jumped a few hurdles, we are still facing each day together. I have often been asked what's the secret to a long relationship and I often answer off-the-cuff "take one day at a time." The reality is that for any relationship to work, you have to love each other but oftentimes love is not enough. Relationships are complicated, they require give and take of both participants, and expectations are rarely met if we are not truly honest with ourselves. It is important to be honest in a relationship but most important, for me anyway, is to be honest with myself. No relationship is perfect, not a single one. But perfection is not the secret; the secret is doing everything you can to try to learn from every situation, respect your life partner, and realize just because you don't think something is important, it most likely is for the other person.

Becoming an Activist

I have always found it amusing that Wally and I are referred to as activists, or in Spanish, "Activista de los derechos de la comunidad de lesbianas, gais, bisexuals y transgéneros." Translated into English it reads "lesbian, gay, bisexual, and transgender (LGBT) community rights activists." It was a label cast upon us before we arrived in the Dominican Republic as if it were a bad thing. I love the Spanish language, despite butchering it like a hog in a bacon factory when I speak it, but it is so much more descriptive and eloquent than English. With rare exception, when someone says something derogatory in Spanish it sounds refined. The truth is that label "activista" was not a label given to us by the cardinal of the Dominican Republic, but one we had earned early in our relationship.

It was late November 1993 and Wally and I were preparing to purchase our first home. I had been working at American Airlines for six years and the flight attendants' union contract had expired and was being negotiated. Progress had been slow and the union was doing everything possible to leverage a new contract to no avail. The union prepared us for a strike, a full-on walkout that would virtually ground the airline. Although I loved my job and certainly didn't have any more than a few months' salary saved, I was willing, along with my colleagues, to walk off the job. The negotiations had gone on too long and American was beginning to implement procedures that violated the contract we were working under. I drove to the Association of Professional Flight Attendants (APFA) union headquarters early the evening of the final deadline for contract negotiations and volunteered to organize and assist anyway I could. We stapled strike signs to large sticks for picketers to carry and communicated with our crews all over the world. It was one of the most organized work actions I had witnessed or ever learned about in school. American Airlines highly under estimated AFPA leadership and their preparedness to execute an organized work action such as a strike.

The strike was to begin at 5:00 a.m. CST so no matter where in the world you were, as a crew member when that time came, you were not to report to work. APFA and American negotiated through the night and somewhere around 3:00 a.m. talks broke off and the strike was called. We loaded the picket signs in the back of volunteers' pickup trucks, who drove them to the DFW airport; I was assigned to the crew resource division and hit the phones. Within a few minutes the phones lit up like Times Square on New Year's Eve.

My first call came from a crew in Idaho Falls to report that they were in solidarity and would not be working the flight; they also informed me that they had taken care of their own transportation home. We were off and running! I stayed on those phones throughout most of the morning. Despite the news reports that American Airlines was disseminating that the strike was a failure and flight attendants were reporting to work in record numbers, we knew that was completely false. Our phone tree was extraordinarily successful, and we were literally tracking every flight and every crew throughout the system. Planes were flying but our resources were informing us that most of those planes were being flown empty. American Airlines realized the financial impact flying empty planes was making, and the two sides negotiated to end the strike.

That November Wally and I earned our label "activist." I include Wally because he never questioned my motives and every step of the way stood by my decision to strike. He joined the committee meetings that I held at our home because I was a phone tree captain and oversaw disseminating information to my assigned colleagues. Communications in 1993 were antiquated by today's norms—there were no cell phones, no internet, no chat apps, no social media, or instant messages. We made old-fashioned phone calls, and we had to be very strategic in our approach. So much for flight attendants just being waiters in the sky.

Along with everyone else, I would have rather avoided a strike and agreed to a contract. The money American Airlines lost would have more than covered the cost of the benefits the union was asking for, but for whatever reason American didn't see it that way. I learned so much being involved in the union preparations for the strike and witnessed up close and personal about how to develop strategy, coordinate volunteers, and motivate membership, that I decided to use my passion in life to continue to provide for those in need. I had a drive and a passion for change. People hate change and people of passion are typically labeled "activist" or "liberal." But both titles I am proud to wear because that means I care for mankind and am concerned about leaving the world a better place than I found it. Our lives as activists began and to this day we do our best to help where we can and raise money for causes we believe in and extend our hands to those organizations that can benefit from our previous experiences.

But not everyone loves an activist, least of all corporate America. I have no doubt that my participation in the strike ruined any opportunity I would have had moving into the corporate arena at American Airlines or any multi-national company at the time. Despite the roadblocks I created in my life, I have no regrets as a result of my activism and would do everything over again exactly the same. I learned a great deal through volunteering, fundraising, and participating in charitable organizations and although I do hope I provided some help and guidance along the way, I am the one who benefited the most. I learned about things I never learned in business school, I matured as a young man, I am still learning the benefits of patience, and I have been truly blessed by the people with whom I have crossed paths along the way. Together with Wally, I will continue to promote change, seek resolutions for those in need, and embrace my passion.

The Windy City

Wally and I spent our first several years together doing what any young couple does—establishing our careers, settling into our routines, volunteering for causes we believed in. By winter 2000, Wally was promoted to a position in his corporate office in Chicago, so we left Dallas behind and moved to the Windy City. For an active Democrat like me it was comparable to moving to the promised land. Chicago is a very progressive city, and its elected representatives are predominately Democrats. Not that I ever really curbed my conversations about politics or issues that I supported, but in Chicago, as a progressive, I never felt that I had to be cautious. In fact, engaging in political conversations was practically a sanctioned sport in Chicago.

Once we got settled and started engaging in the political communi-ty, we immediately became aware of a state senator by the name of Barack Obama. Senator Obama was actually a member of my health club downtown and I would occasionally see him around, although I never met him during those early years of living in Chicago. There was always a lot of buzz surrounding him as the future of Illinois politics, and in 2004 he ran for the U.S. Senate. In July 2004, Senator Obama gave the keynote speech at the Democratic National Conven-tion (DNC) and immediately became a national figure. He easily won his race for the U.S. Senate and was not only a huge celebrity around Chicago but clearly the rising star of the Democratic Party.

I had just launched my career in real estate and was dedicated to making it a success. The real estate market in Chicago was booming and many areas of the city were undergoing renovations. We were living in Lincoln Park, a well-established neighborhood with growing popularity near downtown Chicago. We were ready to move on from our townhome condominium community and the timing was right for us to make a move.

Wally and I really wanted to live in a single-family home without the confinements of a condominium association. We held a jaded view on such associations because of our experience with the president of the condominium association where we lived. Let's just say she was "passionate" about her role and took her job way too seriously—to the point of dumping trash at my front door because I didn't break down my recycling enough to suit her standards. Yes, it was time to go!

We found a beautiful home a few blocks away in the same neighbor-hood we loved. Being in real estate had its advantages—I booked an appointment at the home we would eventually purchase the day it went on the market. Early the next morning we toured the property and when we arrived there were two other couples and their real estate agents also waiting. The listing agent was running a few minutes late so we all stood there awkwardly staring at each other, trying to remain calm. The listing agent arrived and asked if everyone just wanted to look at the same time. We all agreed that would be fine and we entered the property and began to look around.

This home was built circa 1877 just after the great Chicago fire in an Italianate three-level row house style. We entered the main floor and marveled at the impressive architecture—gorgeous original plaster moldings, an original marble fireplace, a newly renovated kitchen (although extremely small by modern standards) greeted us as we walked through the house. We immediately went up to the second floor via the original curved staircase to three bedrooms and found amazing space. It needed to be reconfigured but we felt it had great potential! I don't remember really seeing the lower level of the house because as we were going down the staircase I looked at Wally and said, "We need to make an offer now!"

After taking a very quick look through the street level of the property we went home, and though it was only a few blocks away I felt it took forever. We immediately went to the computer and again I evaluated the pricing for the house, keeping in mind I was new to the business and wanted to keep my emotions out of the transaction. I knew this was a true opportunity. Wally and I had an emotional discussion—I was being emotional, and he was being the standard, level-headed guy he is—and we decided to make an offer. I immediately wrote up the offer, not waiting for my client Wally to change his mind, and walked it back over to the property. I presented a full price offer, no contingencies and with significant amount of earnest money to indicate our seriousness. Keep in mind at this point we had not even put our current home on the market, but I was very confident we could sell quickly.

That was a Saturday morning and the next day there was an open house of another property in our development that was going on the market. Wally suggested we have an open house as well, at the same time as the other property, so we worked all night and the next day we had prepared our home for an open house and had fresh flowers everywhere! I don't remember the specifics, but we had many people come through the property and within two days, it sold! There was a problem as the buyers wanted possession immediately and unfortunately the home we were purchasing was not going to close for 90 days. In the end I paid for their re-location housing cost for a month and both properties closed on the same day. That really kicked off my long and productive career in luxury real estate.

The closings of both properties took place on July 30, Wally's 44th birthday, and we had moved out of our home the day before and spent the night in a hotel. We got up that morning and went to the title company to close on the home we were selling and then a few hours later we purchased our new home. It was truly an exciting day! No more home owner's association, no more stringent rules we had to live with, we could plant flowers anywhere we wanted, and I could recycle freely without fear of retribution.

The New Neighbors

It was about 4:00 p.m. when we arrived at our new house with the moving truck. The movers began unloading our furniture and we both kept running inside and out organizing where everything needed to be placed. All was going very well. It was a beautiful day, the neighborhood was full of people and traffic, the trees were in full bloom, and flowers lined the streets—truly magnificent.

We had been unloading the truck for about an hour when our new neighbors from the house next door came over to introduce themselves. I was completely in shock, not because our neighbors were so friendly and gracious, but because our new neighbors were Moises Alou, the famous Dominican-American baseball player, and his wife Austria. I had met a few celebrities in my lifetime, and although it was always fun meeting famous people, I never in my life thought I would actually live next door to one. Moises Alou, one of the most famous names in baseball and the current prodigy of the infamous Alou baseball dynasty, was my neighbor in my new home. To quote the notable Harry Caray, "holy cow!" I love baseball and I love the Chicago Cubs, and along with every other Cubs fan, I knew the day would come when I would see them win the World Series (little did I know then that I would be living in the Dominican Republic when the Cubs finally won the World Series). It was very surreal as Moises and Austria approached us and extended their hands in friendship and introduced themselves. Later after we exchanged pleasantries, Wally and I retreated inside the house where I fanboyed to Wally about our new neighbors fame! Wally had no idea who Moises Alou was—at the time he barely knew who the Chicago Cubs were—but that would all change in time.

The next evening, we hosted a dinner party at our new home for a few friends, nothing extravagant and in fact I insisted we skip offering dessert as we had way too much to organize just getting everything in its place. Just about the time we were finishing dinner our doorbell rang. It was Austria Alou from next door; there she was standing at my front door with a wonderful Dominican dessert she had prepared for us. The timing could not have been more perfect if planned! Along with the dessert she handed me a wonderful welcome note with all of her and her husband's personal information and the offer if we ever needed anything to please call. It was one of the most gracious expressions of true friendship I have ever experienced, and I still have that card to this day with imprints of *mariquitas* (ladybugs) on the stationery.

Sometimes fate and karma come together and create the most amazing experiences in life and sometimes they create family. The remainder of that summer and early fall Wally and I accepted multiple invitations to attend Cubs games with Austria and her three young boys. We had so much fun and our friendship with the Alou family was instantaneous. As the season ended that year they insisted we visit them in the Dominican Republic for their winter break. Anyone who has ever invited me anywhere knows if it is at all remotely possible I will accept your invitation, so unless you don't want me to show up, don't invite me. Many friends and family have learned this lesson about me over the years.

Having been to the Dominican Republic on several occasions before, I really wanted the opportunity for Wally to visit the country as well and there was no better way than to accept a personal invitation to visit the Dominican Republic than as guests of Moises and Austria. We had a wonderful time and seeing Santo Domingo through the eyes of a local was a completely different experience than visiting as a tourist. The Alous drove us past a few important locations in Santo Domingo—including the National Palace and the U.S. embassy—but for the most part we stuck to visiting the local sights where tourists would not venture. There was no doubt in our minds this would not be our last time in the Dominican Republic.

Obama for President

By 2004 we had been settled in Chicago for a couple of years and had become more involved in the Democratic Party. We had become huge supporters of Senator Obama as well as Senator Dick Durbin, also from Illinois. Contrary to many of their criminal political predecessors, Senators Obama and Durbin were two of the finest U.S. senators our country has ever seen serve in DC. We were thankful that both represented Illinois.

When Senator Obama announced in 2007 that he was running for president, we were all in. He was an amazing senator, he clearly demonstrated outstanding leadership skills, and he was from Illinois. We were very excited as was virtually everyone we spoke to in Chicago; after all, he was our hometown candidate. In 2007 Wally and I were at the peak of our careers and didn't have much surplus time to devote to campaign work, but we did all we could to support candidate Obama for president of the United States. Obama won the Democratic primary. The primary election took longer than usual, as his opponent was Hillary Clinton, and due to huge support for both candidates it wasn't until June 7 that Obama secured enough delegates to win the primary.

Making Dreams a Reality

In winter 2006 we returned to the Dominican Republic to visit the Alous. During this trip we went to dinner and drove past the U.S. embassy in Santo Domingo. Having always been keen about politics and diplomacy, I actually asked them to circle the block, to see the entire compound. As Wally and I returned to Chicago via a connection through Miami, we discussed the future and what our next adventure would look like. We had made the decision to support Barack Obama for president, although at this point he had not made the official announcement, and the idea of being part of his administration was a dream come true. We cleared U.S. Customs and Immigration and made our connecting flight. We had just taken off from Miami on our way to Chicago. I was staring out the window at the twinkle of lights and the Miami Beach high-rise condominiums that passed below and then the plane made a sharp left turn and headed toward Chicago. The sun was setting in the west and as the dark orange of the final sunset cast a glow over the clouds below us I turned to Wally. I remember this clearly. I am not sure what possessed me to turn to him and say, "If you want to be the U.S. ambassador to the Dominican Republic, we could make that happen." I had verbalized an idea that resulted in a conversation that developed into living a dream.

We set out on a journey when we returned home from that trip to the Dominican Republic. We had many conversations about the future of our careers, what the future of our lives together might look like, and the future of our country.

All In

By 2007, we had been living together for seven years. LGBT people had been systematically discriminated against on a daily basis in all aspects of the public and private sector. As a same sex couple, we were not entitled to any legal protections that heterosexual couples take for granted: Wally's insurance at work did not cover me as a spouse, not because I wasn't his spouse but because I couldn't *legally be* his spouse. We couldn't make health care decisions for each other. We couldn't collect each other's retirement. We were not entitled to each other's social security as other married couples were, and in the event one of us died, to remain in the home we bought together, the surviving partner would have to pay inheritance taxes, and as a result would probably have to sell our home.

Wally and I both had been very blessed. We surrounded ourselves with good friends, we both had very supportive families as it related to our relationship, and we both had been fortunate in our careers. The bottom line was, although we were by no means rich, we both made comfortable livings and could afford the benefit of avoiding most discriminatory practices dealt to many others in our LGBT community.

From a very young age I always wondered why some people felt it acceptable to ridicule and demean others for the purpose of validating themselves. I very clearly remember my mother teaching me that we are all human beings, and no one was created better than anyone else regardless of who they were or what they believed. I may not have really understood at the time what she was telling me, but as an adult I often reflect on her words. I couldn't ignore the plight of others, specifically other LGBT people, and I couldn't turn a blind eye toward discrimination.

Wally and I had a political decision to make in 2007. Legal equality was a long-standing fight for the LGBT community. Harvey Milk, Edie Windsor, Larry Kramer, those in the Stonewall riots, and many, many more had sacrificed their safety, livelihoods, welfare, and reputations—and even their lives, such as in the case of Harvey Milk—for gay men and women to have the ability to achieve success and equality. Our decision was really more of an obligation: we owed our community the dedication to continue the quest for equality.

I can respect someone's policy differences on just about any subject with the rare exception of civil rights and human rights. Almost everyone I knew shared the same values as I did: that all people in America should be given the same equal opportunities under the law. It is a pretty basic concept when you think about it. Should there be special laws that apply only to certain classes, demographics, economic positions? Of course not. So if you can't at least come to the table with this basic concept of equality, then we probably don't have much on which to build a friendship. I can respect anyone's opinion to believe differently than me on a policy, but when it comes to basic human rights, we have to start on an equal playing field.

I spent most of my 20s and 30s trying to engage with people of influence who believed that gay people should not be allowed a legal marital union. I engaged in multiple conversations about employers' right to fire employees because they were gay. I protested, I listened, and I expressed my opinions—sometimes diplomatically and sometimes passionately—but I don't believe I ever changed anyone's mind in those one-on-one engagements. I was young, and in retrospect as a more mature person now, I observe very clearly how older people view the opinions of young people. I can be guilty of this myself; however, I have learned some of my biggest life lessons from smart, educated, and engaged young people who care about the future of this country. For someone to be your mentor doesn't necessarily mean they have to be older than you. I am sure there will be critics out there who will say I am imposing my position and not respecting that of others. But at any stage of life, you can't control what others perceive. There isn't anything I can do about others' perception of me. I love my family as much as they love theirs, I love my husband as much as they love their spouses, I love the United States of America, I love democracy and believe it is truly the very best form of government ever created. I will do everything within my power to protect our democracy and promote it throughout the world. Governments work best when its citizens are engaged and have the right to their voices being heard. And that is why Wally and I decided to actively support Senator Obama for president of the United States. Little did we know at the time how life-changing this decision would be for both of us.

Becoming involved in Senator Obama's campaign while living in Chicago was almost expected, everyone who was politically involved was supporting the hometown guy. It was a remarkable experience being involved in a more active manner with the potential presidential candidate. Interestingly, most people didn't realize or may not even know that both candidates were actually Chicago natives. Hillary Clinton grew up in the small community of Park Ridge, located between downtown Chicago and Chicago O'Hare airport. She is as much a Chicagoan as Barack Obama.

Experiencing History in the Making

Leading up to the presidential election in 2008, we were supporting a relatively new man on the political scene. Barack Obama was clearly very notable among the political elite, but he was a local guy. I played tennis at the East Bank Club near downtown and even met him briefly there once. It was electrifying for us to see this regular guy we'd see around town suddenly on this onward trajectory toward the presidency!

We sat in the dining room of our home on Tuesday night, November 4, 2008, with a small group of friends watching the election results throughout the evening. Grant Park in downtown Chicago was packed with people and it was a beautiful Chicago night. Not really being one for huge crowds, Wally and I chose to prepare for what we hoped would be a celebration in our own style. We invited a few friends to our house for a formal dinner where mutually common conversation and friendship could be shared in an environment with grace and dignity regardless of the outcome. The election was without a doubt the most historical thing I would ever see in my lifetime—or so I thought at the time. I had no idea the many historical events I would witness or be an actual part of in the few short years ahead of me.

The weather in Chicago on that early November evening was truly magical, as if it were an ordainment from God that Senator Barack Obama should be president of the United States. (I know God does not ordain presidents—I am a Christian and I believe in God—but I do know He created the world in which we exist and on that night we felt particularly blessed.) We and our guests marveled at the sky, in total amazement that this was early November in Chicago—the clearness in the air, the temperature, the energy! We were just a few short miles from Grant Park, which was packed with people, and the entire city of

Chicago was filled with an energy that was indescribable. It permeated every breath we took that night, and although we were not standing with the hundreds of thousands of others in Grant Park that night, we no doubt felt every ounce of energy they were generating.

As the polls began to close on the East Coast, we were energized, but obviously also anxious about the election! We realized that what was unfolding was a cultural change in the United States that would alter the path of Americans and the world moving forward. I still reflect on that evening and abstractly understand that electing the first African-American as president truly changed the world, but a part of me also understands how sad the world can be when history is measured by the color of a man's skin. Senator Barack Obama wasn't elected to be the first African-American president, he was elected to be president of the United States, who happened to be African-American.

And so there I sat in our home with tears flowing from my face, not because I was sad or excited but because I knew in my heart, at that moment, my life would change forever. I had no doubt that opportunities for so many—me included!—would become more available. Even though at the time Barack Obama did not support same sex marriage, I knew he was a man of intelligence and education, and he would listen and remain open-minded that our cultural needle should move forward, just as I hoped his personal cultural needle would. The United States has seen much change in the past 240 years but for my lifetime, there will be no bigger change than being legally allowed to marry. That would never have happened if not for the leadership of President Obama and Vice President Joe Biden.

I am not sure we even had any real idea what we were celebrating that night. We were just very happy that a new generation was being heard, and happy that the Bush dynasty was over. Beyond that, we were thrilled that an outsider had moved to the inside, and not only to the inside but the leader of the ultimate inside, he was now the president of the United States. There is no greater power or influencer in the political world than the person who sits in the Oval Office. We finished our dinner and polished off all the champagne we had, then joined our friends and neighbors outside. There were people everywhere, walking the sidewalks and greeting each other with smiles and high-fives. We headed to one of our favorite places, Stanley's Kitchen and Tap, to share a celebratory drink, a smile, and a high-five with many of our neighbors. In addition to the crispness in the air that night were also the winds of change, and everyone felt it.

Solidifying Our Decisions

From 2008 to 2010, my real estate business experienced a huge recovery from the burst bubble the industry had suffered in 2007. Wally's career with General Growth Properties, a Chicago-based real estate investment trust and the second largest real estate developer in the United States, had been very successful since our move to Chicago. He had become a senior vice president and eventually an officer of the company. Unfortunately due to some creative financing practices by the CFO, the company declared bankruptcy in April 2009. The family who had started General Growth decades earlier was removed from power. Wally remained throughout most of the bankruptcy and became a member of the executive team that guided the company through the bankruptcy process, but as typical with all public companies that file for bankruptcy, most of the executives eventually depart.

Together we were blessed beyond any expectations we had ever imagined. Fortunately, his executive separation package allowed us some breathing room to make more methodical decisions about our future. During this time we spent a lot of time traveling to the Dominican Republic because we had bought a home on the beach in a new development not far from Santo Domingo. The Alous had become like family to us, and they, too, had bought a home in the same development. It was returning to Chicago from one of those trips that we had a serious discussion about actively pursuing an ambassadorship.

Representing a president of the United States as ambassador to a foreign nation requires at the most basic level a relationship with the president's administration. But developing a relationship with a president doesn't just happen; it requires networking, dedication, and a sincere and genuine interest in serving the American people. We were not really on anyone's radar but there were several people working in the administration we had crossed paths with, so at least we had some access to the White House. We built a consensus of support through our elected representatives and business leaders who knew us and who had access to senior level advisors in the administration. Long before Wally reached a pinnacle in his career in the corporate arena, both he and I had been preparing for this opportunity.

The process one navigates to become a U.S. ambassador from the private sector is complex and requires an unprecedented amount of strategic calculation and execution of a plan that usually is set in place years before. Just like their career counterparts, private sector appointees spend most of their professional lives working on initiatives that benefit democracy and the lives of U.S. citizens. They sit on charitable boards and work with nongovernmental organizations (NGOs) and organizations that conduct mission work throughout the world. They raise money for children's projects and resource centers that serve the marginalized. They volunteer at community centers, participate in local government, and raise awareness for a variety of causes that benefit their communities. They genuinely care about their country and the stabilization of democracy around the world.

Diplomacy and the skills it requires are obtained from a variety of life's experiences, like from the rigid environment of the foreign service, military experience, or a lifetime of service in government. We, however, nurtured our diplomatic skills by navigating private sector complexities and climbing the corporate ladder. We used these skills to work hard in our activist efforts, meeting the right people along the way.

Wally received a call from the White House sometime in early summer 2009 and was asked if he would consider an appointment in Uruguay. At this stage, the situation with Wally's company had become unstable, and change was clearly on the horizon. We took this as a sign that living in Montevideo was meant to be. Unfortunately this appointment never materialized.

Campaigning for Equality

As Wally approached the end of his career with General Growth, we both had become members of the finance committee for Alexi Giannoulias' U.S. Senate campaign. Giannoulias, the former Illinois State Treasurer, was a firm believer in equality for LGBT Americans and did not shy away from the subject matter when asked by the media. He was young, extremely handsome, from a prominent family in Chicago, and had a huge amount of support from the Democratic

Party as he had already won a statewide election. He passed our litmus test: Did he believe in equal rights for all Americans? Would he introduce and support legislation that provided the same legal equal status for LGBT Americans as was provided for heterosexual Americans? The answer was yes.

At this point in our life Wally and I had been in a relationship for 20 years and the campaign for LGBT equality was on the forefront of the news cycle nationally. The LGBT community had grown weary of being second class. We did not enjoy many of the same protections afforded to heterosexual Americans. The LGBT community was tired and so were we. We had supported President Obama and many Democratic candidates in 2008 in hopes that we would finally benefit from the legislative process and that our community would eventually be granted legal equality in the United States.

By late 2010—almost two years into President Obama's first term—it was apparent that our quest for equality was still on the back burner in Congress. The fight had only become more intense and the right-wing opposition was digging in ever stronger to deny gay people the same civil rights as heterosexual Americans. We knew the only way equality was ever going to happen was to elect more legislators who were supportive of the LGBT community to office. When Giannoulias declared his intention to run for the U.S. Senate, we met with him.

Following our first meeting, where he lent support of our community without hesitation, Wally and I immediately became part of his inner finance circle. When we were not working, we were donating virtually 100 percent of our time working to raise money for the campaign. We spent practically every night and every weekend "dialing for dollars" and attending strategy meetings and fundraisers.

Despite our best efforts on the campaign, Giannoulias didn't win. I didn't see it coming. He was a smart, genuine, and a caring young man. I had no doubt he truly cared for the people of Illinois, all the people. His opponent, Mark Kirk, was not a bad person, but he was the incumbent who willfully denied the legal equal rights of his constituents and didn't support the equality of the LGBT community. I just didn't understand in a state like Illinois how Democrats would cross over and support Senator Kirk for re-election.

The 2010 mid-terms were disastrous for Democrats. We lost control of Congress, and I think this took a lot of people by surprise. The truth is we had become apathetic as a Democratic Party. Everyone was living on the high of President Obama being elected and highly underestimated the extreme opposition we faced. We were living in a dream that America had become diverse and that diversity was normal and no longer a qualifier, because we had elected an African-American man as president. But we as Democrats were naïve.

It was the second time I had been personally involved with a U.S. Senate campaign and came out on the losing end. But this was more than just a loss of a single Senate seat. The Democrats lost control of both houses of Congress in that election and overall it resulted in the largest switch of power since the Great Depression. It was beyond devastating for us—it was completely demoralizing. All we wanted was to be equal in the eyes of the law in our own country. Was that really too much to ask for as an American, to be protected equally under our own Constitution?

Wally and I were very concerned about our future as gay men. We had no legal protections, and with Congress being controlled by an anti-LGBT party, we could have been in very serious trouble if President Obama were not re-elected for a second term. Wally had left General Growth just before the mid-term elections and we both decided to dedicate ourselves completely to the Democratic Party in hopes that we could help turn things around in 2012. With his severance package and my income, we were fortunate enough to take a deep breath and decide what was next for us. I'm not exaggerating when I say I was pushing for us to liquidate all our assets and leave the United States for good. I didn't want to be a second-class citizen any longer and as a result of the 2010 midterms I didn't feel there was a future for LGBT people in the United States. Coming off the loss of Giannoulias' campaign could have been devastating to our ambitions for equality, but the fact that we lost control of Congress overshadowed any feelings we had about the loss of that campaign.

Shortly thereafter, fellow Giannoulias supporter Amy Singh asked us to attend a small reception with the newly appointed Chairman of the Democratic National Committee (DNC), Governor Tim Kaine of Virginia. Amy introduced us into the inner circle of the DNC and

Democratic Party politics. We had never been involved with the DNC, so for us it was more informational than anything else as well as an opportunity to meet the person who was being promoted as the future leadership of the Democratic Party.

Becoming National LGBT Co-Chairs for the DNC

The event was held in a small basement room of a restaurant in downtown Chicago. The weather was dreadful when we arrived. The restaurant was located in the center of Chicago's theater district and the place was packed with diners eating before their stage shows began. The reception was very small probably because of the weather and we had the amazing opportunity to speak one-on-one at length with Governor Kaine. That may sound somewhat unimpressive, but anytime you have the chance to exchange political conversation with a sitting governor, especially Tim Kaine, you should take it.

Typically when you attend political receptions, dinners, or events of any kind, you are expected to show up with a check in hand, but on this particular evening it was simply a meet and greet, no contribution expected. Meeting Governor Kaine was beyond motivating for me. He was very personable, genuine, and no doubt in my mind, a very sincere man. He was the consummate politician and I respect him highly to this day. As a result of our meeting, Wally and I decided to become more involved in the Democratic National Committee, including contributing financially as well as becoming active fundraisers. The DNC would play a pivotal role in the re-election of President Obama, so for us it was a natural transition following the Giannoulias Senate race.

In early January 2011 we got a phone call from a young man named Jamie Citron, who most likely saved my faith in the political process. I had been involved in every election cycle since that very first time I handed out "Boren for Senate" flyers when I was 14 years old, but the midterms of 2010 put the final nail in the coffin on my political participation. I was dejected and frustrated. The right-wing extremists had won on the message of hate and bigotry and I heard them loud and clear—they truly hated me and thought I did not deserve to be an equal American. Yes, I took those losses very personally. How else was I supposed to take them?

Jamie was working for the DNC and had heard about our influence and work we had accomplished in the Giannoulias Senate campaign. He wanted us to become involved in the DNC as it prepared for President Obama's 2012 re-election campaign. As a result of his encouragement, we went to Washington, DC, for a DNC meeting with other notable LGBT influencers from around the country. We began preparing a strategy to engage the gay community to ensure President Obama was re-elected.

Governor Kaine's perspective is extremely broad, and he is truly one of the finest human beings I have had the chance to call a friend in my lifetime. Governor Kaine was extremely motivating and positive about the future despite the Democrat's embarrassing defeat in 2010. He motivated us to continue our mission, and shortly after that evening we were asked to be part of a new initiative as National LGBT Co-Chairs of the DNC.

In our new roles, we frequently found ourselves in Washington, DC, meeting with many other LGBT community leaders who held high-level positions of influence in their communities. These were hard working men and women who dedicated large amounts of time and resources to doing everything possible to make the United States a place where LGBT people had the chance to work alongside their fellow citizens without being institutionally discriminated against by the government. I find it curious when the radical right perpetuates this as a position indicating there is some "gay agenda." I assure you the only "agenda" out there is the hope that one day we can all live freely without being legally discriminated against. Nothing more, nothing less, just equal.

Shortly after we joined the DNC as National LGBT Co-Chairs, President Obama announced he would run for re-election and the national campaign office would be located in Chicago. As co-chairs, we all immediately transitioned into Obama For America (OFA) National LGBT Co-Chairs and formed an advisory board that worked directly with the re-election campaign to support President Obama. It was an interesting transition.

The LGBT community, despite progress on many fronts, still experiences a lack of legal protections in the United States. Two of the most significant protections lacking for same-sex couples at the time were the right to legally form a marital union and the right to a discrimination-free workplace. Even as I write this book, one may be legally fired in most states throughout the United States just for being gay. I am not asking for special rights, I am just asking not to be fired for who I am. It is outrageous that one cannot be legally fired for being heterosexual, but at the same time one can be legally fired for being homosexual. America had to overcome these positions of inequality, and President Obama had failed to address these concerns during his first four years in office.

This was a huge hurdle to overcome when fundraising in the LGBT community, and rightfully so in many cases. I was taken to task on more than one occasion when I approached my LGBT sisters and brothers asking them to financially support President Obama's re-elect campaign.

One noteworthy case remains in my mind as a lesson in listening. Wally and I were at a roundtable event for Congresswoman Jan Schakowsky with many notable leaders of the LGBT community in Chicago. There was one couple who had been together even longer than Wally and me, and they were having none of my pitch to support President Obama for a second term. These two women were very strong willed, very smart, very connected, and *very* disappointed that President Obama had failed to provide leadership on equal marriage at this point.

Normally, this would have raised the hair on the back of my neck and I would have defended the president and his policies with all the vigor I could muster. But something guided me to pause and listen. And, boy, did I listen as they emphatically laid out their position, justifying why they had felt betrayed by the president's leadership on the marriage issue. Their concerns were legitimate and, just like Wally and me, they were faced with living their entire lives unequal in their own country. The meeting ended and people left, but I sat there, listening and learning. And one of the most important things I learned was that listening is the art of diplomacy. They not only needed to be heard, they deserved to be heard. We parted ways that night with a handshake. Eventually we met again and they ultimately agreed with me and supported the president. Had I dug in and opposed their position at that initial meeting, I very well could have lost any future opportunity I would have had to gain their support.

There were 10 National LGBT Co-Chairs of Obama For America, and we all directly worked with Rufus Gifford, the National Finance Chair of OFA. Rufus is also gay and an incredible young man on an upward trajectory in government. In fact, Rufus even occupied a spare bedroom in our home for a short time during his transition to Chicago, as did many other national campaign staffers. Our three-level townhome had a separate entrance to the lower level, so we were able to provide a space for campaign staffers in transition. Each and every one of them is a special person who has gone on to contribute to a better world for all of us.

As co-chairs we naturally had divided the country regionally and worked within our spheres of influence to develop a network that allowed us to disseminate information and solicit resources to support the campaign. Equal marriage was a huge hurdle. President Obama was running against Republican Mitt Romney, who had been governor of Massachusetts and was a national figure. Democrats had suffered a huge defeat in the 2010 mid-term elections, and the radical right was highly energized. The future looked bleak and, quite frankly, scared the hell out of me. If Mitt Romney had become president of the United States in 2012, the world would be a very different place for me today.

The 2012 presidential election was extremely personal for me; in fact, it wasn't just about policy, it was about my basic human rights. I once had a conversation with Attorney General of North Carolina Roy Cooper, who is now the governor of North Carolina, at the Waldorf Hotel in Chicago. It was just Attorney General Cooper, a member of his staff, Wally, and me. Attorney General Cooper asked me why we were so passionate about the work we were doing for President Obama, and I remember my words exactly: "If Mitt Romney is elected president of the United States, then I will live my entire life on this earth not being equal in the eyes of my country." It was that simple.

I repeated that message many times to my LGBT brothers and sisters as I traveled the country asking people for money to support the re-election of President Obama. We had to win, we had to step up one more time, the luxury of living on the sidelines no longer existed. And so, for the next 15 months Wally and I dedicated every day to traveling all over the United States. We asked everyone we knew to reach out to their networks to make sure every American citizen they knew would support President Obama in his effort to represent the American people for *four more years*!

3: Experiencing a White House State Dinner

Washington, DC, 2012

Being National LGBT Co-Chairs of the DNC opened many doors for us. We met many influential people in the Obama administration and were extended invitations to further our work. No matter how many times I've visited the White House, it never gets normal, at least not for me. But certain invitations in life affect you in a way that you just can't quite get your head around. Being invited to a White House State Dinner by the president and first lady of the United States is one of them. No one gave us a heads up that we were being extended an invitation. It was completely unexpected and we were thrilled.

In 2012, the only thing I had ever heard about State Dinners was how Michaele and Tareq Salahi, a couple from Virginia, crashed the State Dinner honoring then-Indian Prime Minister Manmohan Singh in 2009. The resulting fallout was that the invitation list to these events was extremely protected, and the security procedures for getting into the White House were increased exponentially.

Arrival Ceremony

The invitation we received was for the State Dinner being held in honor of the then-Prime Minister of the United Kingdom David Cameron. We were then contacted by a staff member at the White House and asked if we would like to attend the arrival ceremony. I had no idea what an arrival ceremony was but of course we accepted—after all it was at the White House.

It was a beautiful morning in DC, and the arrival ceremony would take place on the White House South Lawn. We arrived early but there were already hundreds of people there just wandering around on the South Lawn. It was a bit chilly and there were a few coffee stations, but mostly people were just mingling and visiting with one another. Almost every time we had been to the White House before we had known a lot of people there; this time, we didn't see many familiar faces. The lawn was filled with large contingents of our U.S. Armed

Forces. We saw U.S. and British flags on every light pole, and they had small ones available as souvenirs.

After about an hour of mingling, people began to take their places along the rope line to view the presentation of our military. Not knowing the order of events, I assumed that the president would be arriving soon with the prime minister to give speeches. Sure enough, President Obama, First Lady Michelle Obama, Prime Minister Cameron, and Samantha Cameron, his wife, arrived on the lawn through the ground-level doors and began shaking hands along the rope line. We had been to many events with President Obama and without fail he always made a point to shake hands with his guests. It may sound silly, but we knew we would be seeing the president and the prime minister later that evening, so we maneuvered away from the rope to allow others to greet the president.

President Obama and Prime Minister Cameron took to the podium and delivered some short remarks about the significance of the relationship between the United States and the United Kingdom. There was a crispness in the air. The sun was peaking over the roof of the W Hotel on the east side of the White House and, as if on cue, began reflecting off the brass of the officers' uniforms and metal tips of the flag poles they were holding. The U.S. Armed Forces presented their color guards—the flag bearers, bands, rifle corps, and officers dressed in full military regalia. They stood at attention on the dew-covered grass of the perfectly manicured, green South Lawn of the White House. It was the best of America, and the sense of pride one feels when having the opportunity to observe such an element of American protocol is truly extraordinary. It was one of those "Pinch me, am I dreaming?" moments.

Once the military presentations were complete, the president and the delegation moved to the south portico balcony, and the flags of the 50 United States were presented. The flag-bearers marched in from each side of the portico and then positioned themselves on the curved staircase on each side of the balcony where the official delegation was standing. The flags framed the president and his guests in a fashion that created a picture-perfect presentation of America. I am really not a crier, but if I were, I would have been bawling at this point. It was a beautiful display of patriotism and the best of our diplomacy. Not only was every element perfect, the South Lawn was filled with a cross-section of Americans and British—straight, gay, black, white, native, men, women, transgender—a true representation of all both our countries had to offer.

Dinner Is Served

That evening, we arrived at the White House guest entrance across the street from the W Hotel Washington, DC. It was amazing to see everyone in formal gowns and tuxedos moving across President's Park into the secure areas where we were screened before entering the east entrance of the president's home.

When guests arrive at the White House for events hosted by the president and the first lady, they enter via the east side portico through two large doors into a reception hall. From the reception hall, a long hallway leads past the White House theater on one side and a beautiful garden on the other, overlooking the South Lawn. Just past the theater, guests enter into a reception area where the media are located. I had not expected to see the media, but then again I had never been to a State Dinner. As we entered the reception area, our names were announced and a flurry of camera flashes lit up the room. It was blinding and I remember lifting my hand up to the side of my face. I now understand why celebrities where sunglasses all the time on the red carpet when arriving at the Oscars! Sadly, I was never able to obtain a copy of any picture the media took of Wally and me that night. Past the reception area, guests enter the original lower level of the White House hall, which has a beautifully groin vaulted ceiling and is flanked by women's and men's lounges on each side. We proceeded up a flight of wooden stairs with a beautiful brass rail to the formal foyer of the White House facing Lafayette Park.

At the top of the stairs, we were greeted by a military band and several servers with silver trays of champagne! It was an incredible evening as we were allowed to wander freely throughout the first floor of the White House and visit with all the other attendees. This particular State Dinner was larger than most primarily because of our close ties to Great Britain. Among the approximately 300 guests that evening were the cast of *Downton Abbey*, many U.S. senators, current and former ambassadors, notable businessmen and businesswomen, and many dignitaries from Great Britain. At the time I didn't know many people in attendance and I had never heard of *Downton Abbey*, although that changed shortly afterward. But one notable guest I recognized standing alone was Sir Richard Branson.

I have always been fascinated with space travel and I had read about Branson's project of developing an aircraft that could carry people into space. I introduced myself and it turned out to be one of the most intriguing conversations I had had in my life. I found him to be extremely engaging and generous with his time. He spoke at length about his project and other matters of interest. I was truly in awe of the evening and the people I was surrounded by. I just couldn't believe I was at a State Dinner.

After an hour or so of mingling the guests began to form a receiving line to meet the president and first lady of the United States and their honored guests, the prime minister of the United Kingdom and his wife. We had been through these receiving lines before, but every time it only becomes more exciting. We usually tried to position ourselves in the line with people we knew in order to share the experience, but this particular evening we really didn't know that many people.

As we approached the front of the line, a White House military member greeted us and took our announcement card that we received when we entered the White House. Then before we greeted the president, a member of the military announced us. Believe me, it never gets old hearing your name being announced and seeing the president of the United States turn, extend his hand, and flash you a huge smile. At that point President Obama turned to us and said...well, I couldn't possibly remember exactly what he said, but whatever it was made us feel as if we were the only people in the room.

We were especially excited because a very close friend of ours had called Wally earlier in the day to mention a friend of his, Bea, was very close friends with Prime Minister Cameron and his wife. They even considered her one of their adopted daughters. Bea had just spent the previous month with prime minister and his wife, and our friend instructed Wally to be sure and give a big hello to the prime minister from Bea. Perfect! An ice breaker! After all what do you say to a prime minister you have never met? So, after our announcement, Wally proceeded first and greeted President Obama and the first lady. Fortunately, at this point we had met both of them multiple times, so our greetings were warm and appropriate, but as Wally moved forward to greet the prime minister, I was talking with First Lady Michelle Obama but noticed out of the corner of my eye that Prime Minister Cameron was giving Wally a very strange look. We moved through the line and out the doors of the south portico, down the curved staircase to the South Lawn. We then proceeded to the tented pavilion where the dinner would take place.

The next morning our friend called Wally again and this time apologized for a most egregious diplomatic faux pas. Apparently, our friend thought we were meeting the prime minister of *Cameroon* with whom Bea was very close friends, not Prime Minister *Cameron* of the United Kingdom. No wonder the prime minister gave my husband a look as if he had truly lost his mind!

The evening could not have been more majestic. That night we had the privilege to hear, up close and personal, John Legend perform in an intimate setting with just him and a piano, followed by the British band Mumford & Sons. I had never heard of Mumford & Sons, but that night I became a huge fan.

The entire evening was surreal and I often reflect on the people who were in attendance that evening. At the time, I could only imagine how a guest list for an event of this caliber comes together. I would learn all too well, while serving President Obama in the Dominican Republic, the complications and intricacies that go into organizing something as important as State Dinner. I sat next to Richard Wolffe, a notable British-American journalist who has written several books about the Obama White House. I have always had an addiction to journalism, most likely because my passion for politics, but I love how a person can formulate our language into a story that allows a reader to experience a scenario without actually being there. Journalists do that every day—they deliver the facts but they also allow you to experience those facts. For me, sitting next to a journalist like Richard was phenomenal; I am not so sure he would say the same, as I am sure I labored him with questions about his profession the entire evening.

During our time at the State Dinner we had the opportunity to see Health and Human Services Secretary Kathleen Sebelius, whom Wally and I had met previously. Next to our table was Senator John

Kerry, who was soon to become the Secretary of State. The list goes on and on. During one of the meal's courses, Secretary Sebelius brought her dear friend Senator Claire McCaskill to meet us.

There are a lot of amazing women in this world, but there is no one I admire or respect more than Senator McCaskill, and I am honored to be able to call her a friend. We all clicked immediately. Wally and I held an event for her campaign in our home in Chicago shortly after meeting her. The next year, she attended Wally's official swearing-in as the U.S. ambassador to the Dominican Republic and a few years later she visited us in the Dominican Republic while celebrating her birthday. Another of her visits took us all to our dear friend Marc Anthony's house for an afternoon beverage.

There was a time in my life when I never would have been open to the idea of exposing myself to these opportunities. When you grow up in a small town, you're often told big cities are places where scary people go so they can be anonymous. You end up being scared of your own shadow, or at least that was my impression. It was through education and my ultimate desire to explore political ambitions that finally led to me realizing that my mother's words were true: People are just people, we are all the same. Yes, there are people with more money, more physical beauty, more influence, but despite the attributes some people are blessed with, they are really no different than any of us. For the most part, regardless of our position in life, we all strive for family, friendship, stability, peace, health, and happiness. These are the common factors that drive the bond of humanity, and my friends Claire and Marc are no different. I am as blessed to have so many wonderful people in my life whose names will never appear on a marquee but are every bit as important to me.

That evening as we left the State Dinner, we lingered a bit, walking as slowly as possible up the south side of the White House toward the east exit. The evening sky was illuminated by the surrounding lights of the city and the White House was surrounded by a glow of landscape lighting reflecting off the pureness of its white paint. The air was brisk and fresh and smelled of freshly cut grass. We meandered for no other reason than wanting to take in every second possible in that environment. Dressed in our formal tuxedoes, we almost felt completely alone. As I slipped my arm into Wally's as we slowly walked toward the exit, I never felt safer. Not because we were surrounded by the best security on earth, but because hope prevailed in my heart. I actually had the privilege of having hope for the future of our country and the equality of our people. Democracy was good and our country was on a beautiful path with a future to peace, prosperity, and inclusion for all Americans.

4: Navigating the Waters of a Diplomatic Appointment

Since President Obama's first administration, Wally had been inspired to seek an appointment as an ambassador. Becoming an ambassador is a long process, almost like gardening. You plant small seeds, nurture them, and watch them grow into a blossoming flower. We spent much time working on campaigns and volunteering, and attending receptions and dinners, all the while talking up Wally's qualifications and why he would be an excellent ambassador. We both had been successful in the private sector and felt we were at a plateau in our careers. The time had come to push forward and see where the path would lead.

After the campaign and the inauguration in January 2013, Wally and I took a month off and traveled throughout Asia and Australia with our dear friend Austria Alou. We wanted to get away from life for a bit, re-collect our thoughts, and focus on the future. Wally had made his ambitions known to those of influence in the Obama world, but beyond that there wasn't really much more to be done. We were not insiders, we had not served in President Obama's first administration, and we were certainly not on first name basis with many of those who knew the president personally.

We had an incredible trip to China, Australia, and New Zealand. In fact, we weren't the only ones who needed to reboot; while sitting at a café in Auckland, a member of the Obama campaign with whom we had worked closely strolled past and we ended up sharing a fun few days together reminiscing. The world is a small place.

Deflated "the call" didn't come while we were on our trip, we flew home from Australia with the resolution that it was time to focus on new adventures. We had resigned ourselves that an ambassadorship was not in the cards, but we could take personal pride in the fact we had secured our opportunity for equality in the next four years.

The Call

Months later, I had been in Europe, and when I returned to O'Hare airport, Wally was waiting. We were driving home, and the conversation was typical: How was your flight? How was the weather in Europe? And so forth. And then Wally began to cry. Wally has always been a crier; it is actually very genuine and wonderful to watch another human being be so open and transparent with his feelings. But he was driving and the I-90 interstate was bumper-to-bumper traffic; I was afraid he was going to rear-end someone if he didn't calm down. He collected himself and told me about the phone call from Air Force One.

He began with "I got the call!" My initial reaction was, "What call?"

Wally told me that he had received a blocked call on his phone and he was hesitant to answer it. You see, when you raise money for as many political candidates and charitable organizations as we have over the years, a blocked call is not one you usually answer. He told me he had a feeling based on the time of day and for some reason he answered. A voice on the other end asked if this was Wally Brewster, and when he responded yes the voice informed him it was Air Force One and to please hold for the president of the United States!

A few moments later Valerie Jarrett came on the line and told him she was with President Obama and wanted to discuss his interest in serving the president's administration as the U.S. ambassador to the Dominican Republic. No doubt that type of call would catch anyone off guard. I don't care who you are, when the president of the United States asks you to join his administration it isn't something you really have to think about.

The call was three minutes long, and obviously Wally was very excited to join the administration. Valerie informed him someone from the White House would be in touch and they exchanged pleasantries and ended the call. Wally still has the screenshot of the call from Air Force One as a memento on his phone, which simply says "Blocked Caller" and the timestamp: March 15, 2013, 10:14 a.m.

I would have given anything to have been there at the time, to have been privy to his reaction and the pride he must have been feeling.

But life allowed Wally the opportunity to experience something that special all by himself. Although I may have missed out on a shared moment with the person I love more than life itself, I will always be thrilled he was able to absorb that pride without it being interrupted. That was a life-changing phone call that redirected our path in life forever.

The Vetting Process

The other dynamic of the call was Wally was asked not to tell anyone he was under consideration for the nomination. He was informed there was a vetting process and once that was completed the president would make a formal announcement. In the meantime, he was to please wait for the call from the White House legal counsel. It was early April when a lead investigator from the FBI reached out to Wally and informed him he would be conducting his interview and background investigation in preparation for his ambassador appointment.

I would suspect that anyone would be somewhat nervous knowing that the FBI was going to start digging into their past. We have all seen television dramas where the FBI springs forth with a "gotcha moment." There were no gotcha moments in our past; we had lived all of our lives rather transparently, but it was an interesting and exciting process. The lead investigator was a very nice man who had decades of experience in the FBI and assured Wally he would keep him informed every step of the way. We were also reminded every step of the way that the process was to remain confidential.

This is the part that got tricky. We had to compile a list of every person we ever traveled with outside of the United States for the past 20 years. Wally and I had traveled the world, and we loved traveling with friends so practically every place we ever traveled, we traveled with someone. The FBI needed their contact information in addition to certain vital information that I didn't have access to without personally asking them, which would obviously raise questions. I had to call more than 100 people and ask them for information, such as their legal name on their birth certificate, their dates of birth, social security numbers, names of their children, and email addresses. All I could tell them is Wally was under consideration for a position with the government and someone would be contacting them for references.

I think it was obvious to our friends and family what was going on and everyone cooperated very professionally without pressing for information. Shortly after supplying the list to the FBI, the investigators began contacting them one by one. It didn't matter where they lived—they were contacted. Some people reached out after they spoke with the FBI to inform us they had been interviewed, and some did not. Those who did really didn't discuss what was asked, except that they were asked to provide three more people they knew that had a relationship with us personally or professionally. It was similar to a tree branch spreading into other branches; as the tree grew, this exercise kept going until no new contacts were provided.

In addition to the FBI vetting process, we filled out an extraordinary amount of paperwork. Literally hundreds of documents had to be completed, witnessed, and even notarized. On the advice of former employees who had worked in the government, we hired legal counsel to ensure all the documents were completed correctly. This was wise advice. Patrick Croke was a good friend and an associate with Sidley Austin in Chicago, the firm where President Obama had practiced law prior to his political career. Patrick is an amazing young man, extremely smart, and very well educated at Georgetown and Harvard. He also was well connected in the government community and was able to quickly resolve any confusion with our vetting process. He crossed all the t's and dotted all the i's, allowing our process to move forward efficiently.

The other part of the process that was relatively simple for us was the review of our financial records. I have learned that some people have very complicated financial lives—we're not among them, thankfully. I can't tell you the number of clients I engaged with in the real estate business who sometimes could not write a simple check, not because they didn't have money—they had lots of money—but because the money was invested or involved in a trust or some other complicated financial instrument that required legal intervention. Sometimes being rich can be difficult, I call these difficulties RPP's (rich people problems). Wally and I kept our financial lives somewhat simple. The only obstacle that raised a red flag was we at one time were part owners in a thoroughbred race horse named Go On With It Son. We raced him professionally and we won a few races. We didn't profit from him because we learned in the process that horses eat a lot, require health care and adequate boarding, and in general are very expensive investments. This seemed to raise some levels of concern because the horse racing business tends to attract some unsavory characters. Fortunately, our partners in the horse were legitimate horse owners and had been in the business for a long time. Our partnership in our horse was squeaky clean and it didn't take long for investigators to sort out any concerns they may have had with our ownership. We were required to file 10 years of tax returns—unlike the current president who refuses to allow the American people transparency into his financial life. We had the same accountant all those years, so those records were readily available.

Once the FBI background checks were completed and our report was submitted to the White House legal counsel, we were scheduled to attend the Ambassador Training Seminar at the Foreign Service Institute.

Receiving Enlightenment

It was during the Ambassadorial Training Seminar that we first learned of Cardinal Nicolás de Jesús López Rodríguez. He had been serving as the cardinal of the Dominican Republic for more than 35 years when Wally was appointed by President Obama in 2013 to serve as the U.S. ambassador to the Dominican Republic. The cardinal was the highest-ranking official of the Catholic Church in the Western Hemisphere and wielded unheard-of power over the culture, civil society, and the government of the Dominican Republic. He was not a nice man and shortly thereafter we would find out just how not nice he was when the official announcement of Wally's nomination was published.

The Ambassadorial Training Seminar was an enlightening experience for both of us. The State Department included spouses and partners in this experience as it provided them with an opportunity to get an image of what their lives might be like for the next three to four years. Although it was validating to be included in the training seminar, there wasn't much reality exposed regarding the position of the spouse of an ambassador. I can appreciate the diplomatic approach that was taken during the seminar, but as it related to spouses it would have been much more helpful to have just heard the truth about what the experience was going to reflect. In retrospect it is possible they didn't know what the truth would look like for each spouse.

We attended the seminar with career diplomats who had spent their entire adult lives serving the American people in foreign countries with occasional assignments stateside and with nominees from the private sector that in many cases had never lived in a foreign country. The balance between the private and public sector provides a unique opportunity for both sides to share insights and experiences. It is still one of the fondest memories I have during the preparation process because it provided us a sense of inclusion and participation.

As the seminar continued, the White House would release to the press the names of the ambassadors who had been nominated to various countries based on the receipt of their *agrément* from the host country. U.S. ambassadors are nominated by the president of the United States to serve as his personal representative to a foreign country, but the foreign country or host nation as termed by the State Department must agree to the nomination. The process of agreement is described by the French word *agrément*. After all, the host nation is receiving you as a guest in their country.

One by one, the ambassador nominees in our seminar would receive notification when their *agrément* was accepted and the White House would release to the press their official nomination. But as the days continued to pass, the *agrément* for Wally's nomination to the Dominican Republic was not returned. We all have an intuition, and mine was telling me something was amiss. We began to make inquiries with our State Department counselor about the process, only to be reassured all was fine. These processes can be bureaucratic in nature and can take time, they told us. But the days kept passing and the silence grew louder. Finally, I insisted Wally call the White House to inquire if they had been informed of any challenges with his *agrément*. And indeed, they had information, and that information was not good.

The Dominican Republic is a democratic nation in the Caribbean that shares its island nation border with Haiti. Although a democracy, the Dominican Republic is deeply rooted in Catholic principles and Cardinal Rodríguez was involved in all things government when it comes to Dominican politics.

The cardinal caught wind of the fact that President Obama had selected an openly gay man to serve as U.S. ambassador. This did not sit well with the cardinal, and he was insisting that the Dominican Foreign Ministry deny the *agrément*. The Vatican has refused to accept multiple nominees as U.S. ambassador to the Vatican, but it is extraordinarily rare for a country that maintains a bilateral relationship with the United States to deny the *agrément* of their partner country's ambassador nominee.

Wally and I had just sat down at the Jefferson Hotel in Washington, DC, just a few blocks north of the White House, to meet with Chad Griffin, Human Rights Campaign president, when Wally got a call from the White House legal counsel. Wally was told of the situation and was asked to be patient as the White House was addressing the issue in the Dominican Republic regarding his acceptance as the U.S. ambassador. Although they would not confirm the specifics of the challenges with Wally's *agrément*, they did confirm there were challenges that were being addressed with the utmost diligence. As unnerving as this news was, it was just another hurdle in the process over which we had to jump. The next afternoon, the *agrément* from the government of the Dominican Republic had been accepted. I doubt we will ever know what communication really took place between the Dominican Republic Foreign Ministry and our State Department and White House. At that point, though, neither of us really cared; we were just elated we were one step closer to moving to the Dominican Republic.

During our tenure in the Dominican Republic we had the opportunity to develop a great friendship with the former acting Foreign Minister of the Dominican Republic at the time all of this occurred, Jose Manuel Trullols and his wife Yslem. I can assure you based on that friendship, it was not the government of the Dominican Republic that was objecting to my husband's appointment.

This was only the beginning of our tumultuous non-relationship with the cardinal and the Catholic Church. Following the official press release from the White House nominating my husband as the U.S. ambassador to the Dominican Republic, Cardinal Rodríguez held a press conference the following Sunday after mass in Santo Domingo. In this televised speech, he referred to Wally as a *maricon*—that's "faggot" to the non-Spanish speaker. This is just about the worst slur one can use to refer to gay person; it is extremely vulgar and shouldn't be in the vocabulary of anyone claiming to be a Christian let alone a priest. But it didn't stop there. The cardinal's close friend and ally Vicar Pablo Cedano, in the same press conference, criticized the nomination as "a lack of respect" and warned Wally, "If he arrives, he'll suffer and will be forced to leave." This was a blatant threat made on live television.

We proceeded with our plans anyway. We had worked too hard and come too far to stop now.

Black Monday Protest

After the cardinal made his opening comments about Wally's nomination, the religious community attempted a poorly organized protest against him on July 15, 2013, dubbed Black Monday. I was concerned about this because it was getting a lot of press at the time and we were very concerned this could adversely impact Wally's ability to get confirmed by the U.S. Senate.

I called a dear friend in the Dominican Republic the day after and asked her if the protest had been successful in her opinion. She laughed and responded to me that no one listens to that man, referring to the cardinal, and certainly no Dominican was going to wear black all day to protest someone they didn't even know. The whole thing was a bust. Following the cardinal's initial comments and attempt at the Black Monday protest, things calmed down pretty quickly, but not for long.

During our tenure in the Dominican Republic the cardinal would frequently comment about public appearances or initiatives of the embassy. He criticized us for inviting members of the LGBT community organizations to our home. He criticized us for supporting Gay Pride Month and raising the rainbow flag at the ambassador's residence. This made the front page of the newspaper and created a small amount of buzz around town, but it didn't stop community support from our allies. He criticized us for accepting invitations to speak at schools about government service and U.S. democracy. The man didn't have a positive word to say about anyone, us even less so.

There is so much you do not learn at the Ambassadorial Training Seminar and some things to be fair they can't teach you. A clear-laid path of how to be an ambassador or how to be an ambassador's spouse does not exist, so there are some experiences that just must be faced head on and you are trusted to have the foresight to deal diplomatically with those experiences, otherwise it is doubtful the president of the United States would have asked you to take the job in the first place.

Something that was not discussed in the seminar was the dynamics of the Diplomatic Corps. The Diplomatic Corps is an organization of all foreign diplomats serving in a host country. Typically the longest serving diplomat is designated as the Dean of the Diplomatic Corps with rare exception, and one of those exceptions was the Dominican Republic. The Dominican Republic democracy has difficulty separating its religious influence from its government positions; the papal nuncio is the de-facto Head of the Diplomatic Corps in the Dominican Republic. Interestingly, the papal nuncio, the Vatican ambassador to the Dominican Republic, had arrived only a few short weeks prior to my husband, and was surrounded by a controversy himself. He had been sent to the Dominican Republic to replace the former papal nuncio, who had been accused of molesting children and had fled the country. Nonetheless, his position provided him the senior rank among the foreign diplomats. This meant that anytime there was an event hosted by any member of the Diplomatic Corps the papal nuncio would be present and technically preside over the event as the senior diplomat.

We had little control over the actions of these so-called religious leaders, so we forged ahead with what we had been working on so hard for so long—for Wally to become ambassador. But first we had to jump the next hurdle in Wally becoming ambassador—his Senate confirmation.

5: A Confirmation Hearing, a Lockdown, and a Wedding

Wally's Eventful Senate Confirmation

Following the Ambassadorial Training Seminar, Wally continued with briefings at the State Department and various agencies that had representatives at the U.S. embassy in Santo Domingo. I returned to Chicago and started preparations for our move with brief trips back and forth to DC for various functions. When Congress returned to Washington following their Fourth of July recess, some of our friends' confirmation hearings with the Senate Foreign Relations Committee were being scheduled.

The confirmation process requires a hearing before the Senate Foreign Relations Committee, and then, if approved by the committee, nominees are sent to the full Senate for a confirmation vote. Unfortunately for Wally, Senator Bob Menendez, then chair of the Foreign Relations Committee in 2013, would not allow any ambassador nominees in the Western Hemisphere to be scheduled for a hearing. Senator Menendez was not in agreement with President Obama regarding the failed Cuban policies of previous administrations and wanted to influence how the White House was going to move forward with opening up relationships with Cuba.

Anyone with an eighth-grade civics education knows that foreign policy is determined by the executive branch—the president—not a single U.S. senator. But Senator Menendez thought that by keeping the president's ambassadorial appointees from moving forward, he could force President Obama into allowing him to influence and control the policy regarding Cuba. This tactic delayed Wally's nomination hearing.

This added to Wally's personal hardships; his father was terminally ill and it was just a matter of time before he died. Like any good son, Wally wanted to tell his father that he had been confirmed as the U.S. ambassador to the Dominican Republic. It was extremely important to him because his mother had passed away many years earlier. This information was conveyed to Senator Menendez; his response was that he did not care. Through a huge effort from other political support, an agreement was reached with the senator—only for Senator Lindsay Graham to place a hold on all nominees! I understand that these bureaucratic options can be used in a positive manner for the benefit of the American people in legislative matters; however, they were being used manipulatively against Wally.

Senator Menendez used his position to block my husband's hearing for very personal reasons. He of all people knew this was wrong, yet he held hostage the career of a man who spent his life supporting the initiatives of the Democratic Party—ironically Menendez's own party. And as for Senator Graham, well, we will never know the reason he released his hold on Wally. But we do know the confirmation never would have happened if not for the efforts of Senator Durbin and his staff. We are eternally grateful for his efforts and support during that exhaustive experience.

Wally finally was scheduled for his hearing on October 3, 2013. We prepared every day for the hearing. Wally attended briefings at the State Department, many of which I was allowed to attend, save for those where confidential or classified conversations would take place. It was good I was able to provide him with an extra set of ears. I would constantly ask him questions about the information he was provided so that he would be as prepared as possible for his confirmation hearing. We went to bed early the night before the hearing and felt comfortable we had checked every item in the list, crossed every t and dotted every i.

The next morning, we woke to a beautiful day in DC; we couldn't have felt better. We met Wally's team at the State Department, and were escorted to the parking garage where two white non-descript vans awaited to drive us to Capitol Hill. The staff who had prepared Wally for this big day carried boxes full of briefing material. At the time I was curious why so much material was to accompany us, but this was a reflection of the process the State Department goes through to be prepared for every hurdle it might face.

We arrived at the Senate Foreign Relations Committee briefing room, which is attached to the hearing room. We were greeted by the Foreign Relations Committee staff and several senators who were already there to participate in the hearing. The plan of the day was that Senator Tim

Kaine would introduce Wally to the committee because we had a long history of working with him at the DNC. Senator Durbin, our senior ranking senator from Illinois, would provide the closing speech.

The Lockdown

As we waited for the remaining senators to arrive to start the hearing, an alarm sounded in the building. Most people don't react to alarms in big public buildings because in most cases someone accidently triggers the alarm by opening an emergency exit door. But this was no accident. The flat-screen television in the briefing room started blinking red and notified us the entire building was on lockdown. We were instructed to lock all doors, not go in or out, remain away from windows, and close all blinds. The administrator in the briefing room answered a call and quickly informed everyone that this was not a drill—there was an active shooter and the Capitol Police were in pursuit. Shit got real very fast.

As prepared as we were, we'd never anticipated an active shooter. I looked at Wally and just shook my head. By the time this was happening, Senator Tom Udall indicated he was not going to cancel this hearing. This would be the first hearing he was to chair for the Foreign Relations Committee, and he wasn't going to allow an active shooter to stand in the way. Senator Sheldon Whitehouse and Senator Durbin were also there with us, but we still needed a few others to show for the hearing to proceed, and with the lockdown in place, nobody was permitted to leave their present location. Senator Kaine eventually made it to the briefing room and there were enough senators present to proceed.

We were allowed to enter the hearing room through the connecting door, and everyone took their places. The hearing room was completely full because, well, nobody could leave because of the lockdown. It was surreal to watch my husband along with nominees Brian Nichols, a career diplomat nominated to be U.S. ambassador to Peru, and the Honorable Roberto Moreno, a California judge nominated to be U.S. ambassador to Belize, face the members of the committee. At the last minute, Senator John McCain arrived, obviously unhappy and anxious. The only question he seemed to care about asking Wally was if he had ever been to the Dominican Republic. Clearly, his staff had not briefed him well. It left me reeling that he was challenged in finding an appropriate question to ask my husband.

The nominees were seated at a small table in chairs that were too low for the table and positioned in a way that they were forced to sit close to the table. They faced the committee members, who were seated on the dais in large leather chairs in front of a stately wood-carved wall. It was intimidating to me, but Wally was confident in his preparations and did not seem concerned.

The hearing didn't last long, and we got out quickly. Wally was fortunate. Other nominees were not so lucky. These hearings are a chance for senators to go on record voicing concerns, and typically these concerns are not so diplomatically expressed.

Senator Durbin's closing remarks on Wally's behalf were heartfelt and moving:

> I am here today in enthusiastic support of your nomination. We both know there is some controversy already associated with it in terms of sexual orientation, and your partnership with Bob. You have spent a lifetime dealing with this issue, at least your adult lifetime dealing with this issue, and now we both know as Ambassador it appears you will be dealing with it after confirmed in a foreign land, the Dominican Republic. Tell me how you view this as you go forward. The President is behind you, I'm behind you. How do you and Bob view this as you have this opportunity to serve representing the United States?

Wally answered how proud he was to be an American and serve the American people. He recognized no matter the task, life has its challenges, and he would be proud to move the initiatives of the American people forward representing them in the Dominican Republic.

Senator Durbin responded, "You could have walked away when the controversy started and neither of you would. I respect you so much for that, I think you are going to advance the cause of human rights in ways that many people never dreamed of given this opportunity, so I wish you both the very best."

Senator Udall closed the hearing with comments regarding the sacrifices spouses and partners make on behalf of their families in supporting these nominations. I never expected to be recognized in this process, because typically that just isn't how life works. I was grateful for the personal recognition by Senators Durbin and Udall, and I took their words to heart. I worked to support my husband's initiatives every single day he served in the Dominican Republic.

When I reflected on that afternoon, my thoughts vacillated from frustration to sympathetic understanding. I could never have prepared for an active shooter. I was frustrated and angry that we were controlled by the situation and at one point even felt happy it was over. I had never considered that someone had died. What we eventually learned was the suspect rammed the White House gate and led the police on a chase through DC, only to die in a shoot-out in front of the building where we were. The suspect, Miriam Carey, was a dental hygienist from Connecticut. What the police didn't know at the time is she did not have a weapon in the car and her small child was in the back seat. A tragedy, indeed.

My frustration that day precluded any thoughts I had for the family who lost a loved one or what instigated a young woman to lose her life and risk the life of her child. I had somehow made it all about me, but I came to realize that although I was affected, it wasn't all about me. The fact is, it is never about just us. There is always something more impactful taking place around us. October 3 will always be a day that frustrated and created anxiety for me. But for the family of Miriam Carey, that will forever be the day their loved one lost her life and her child lost a mother. We will never know what prompted Miriam to drive her car into the White House gate and flee the scene. I learned a lesson that day: no matter how rough things might look in the moments in which we are challenged, someone in that same moment is facing a much greater hurdle.

The Final Hurdle

Following the hearing, the committee has the opportunity to forward follow-up questions or clarifications to the nominees, and then will vote to send their nomination to the full Senate for approval. On November 14, 2013, we got a call from our dear friend Pat Souder that

Senator Durbin was successful in getting Wally's nomination on the Senate docket for that afternoon. This was the last opportunity before Thanksgiving break—otherwise it might be sometime in January 2014 before his nomination could be considered.

We watched with great anticipation on C-Span as Senator Harry Reid called for Wally's nomination without objection. Senator Jeanne Shaheen banged her gavel and confirmed Wally's nomination without objection. This meant that Wally was confirmed by the U.S. Senate as the Extraordinary and Plenipotentiary United States Ambassador to the Dominican Republic His Excellency James Walter Brewster, Jr. Now that is one heck of a title!

We both wanted to proceed with the swearing-in process as quickly as possible, primarily because we had been without a permanent residence and had been living in Florida temporarily. Once the vetting process had been completed and we attended the Ambassador Training Seminar, we were feeling relatively comfortable the confirmation process would move forward. There were not any personal dynamics that would have raised any controversy with Wally's confirmation. Yes, we had been involved extensively in the Democratic Party but that was typical. Democratic administrations typically appoint fellow Democrats, just like Republican presidents nominate ambassadors or other cabinet members who are usually active Republicans. It was complete, or so we thought. The final obstacle left had been Senate confirmation.

Underestimating the time a confirmation would take, we sold our home in Chicago—quickly, as it was in a premium location and we had taken exceptional care of it—to avoid having a second property to rent. We still owned and rented our Texas home. I wasn't fond of being a landlord to even one rental property, much less two, so the last thing I wanted while living in the Dominican Republic was the distraction of multiple rentals. The problem, though, was we were left with no place to live! Once again Austria Alou came to our rescue. The Alous owned a home in Fort Lauderdale they were not living in permanently and offered to lease us a room in the house. So we were off to Florida as we waited for the Senate to vote on Wally's nomination. Following the vote, we flew to DC the next day and began preparations for Wally's swearing-in and our wedding.

Oh yes, we were getting married, too.

The Swearing-In

We had spoken with Vice President Biden's office about conducting Wally's swearing-in. We had been close to the vice president and his staff ever since the re-election, and we respected him greatly. The only date he was available in DC to conduct the swearing-in was November 22, 2013. That gave us only eight days to plan! If an active shooter on Capitol Hill wasn't going to keep Wally's hearing from happening, certainly an accelerated time span wasn't going to keep us from getting Wally sworn-in as ambassador and us getting legally married.

There are two types of being sworn in and two types of weddings: the legal and the ceremonial. Each is complicated and requires coordination, but the ceremonial aspects are extremely difficult and short time frames tend to create major hurdles.

Wally was officially sworn-in as the ambassador in Senator Durbin's office on Capitol Hill. Senator Durbin's office once had been occupied by President Abraham Lincoln, and a portrait of the former president hangs in that office. Our dear friend Senator McCaskill attended, along with our friend Congresswoman Jan Schakowsky. It was a very special moment, and we invited our good friends Nan Schaffer and Karen Dixon to join us. With the small gathering watching, Jennifer Wicks of the State Department administered the legal oath of office to Wally.

We had a brief celebratory drink afterward, and then we went back to work preparing for our move to the Dominican Republic. But we still had to get legally married first. During the next 48 hours, we were consumed with getting invitations prepared for the ceremonial swearing-in and our wedding.

None of this would have happened without the consummate professionalism of Vice President Biden's staff, who were so helpful in processing our guest list for admission to the White House. Wally's ceremonial swearing-in was held at the Indian Treaty Room in the Eisenhower Executive Office Building adjacent to the White House. Every guest had to submit personal vital information in 72 hours or they would not be able to attend the swearing-in.

Despite inviting half the world to attend, we assumed only 30 to 40 close friends and family would show up due to the short timing. Well, we were wrong. We had 175 people respond that they would be there, and this put a burden on all involved in the coordination of the events.

Our Wedding, Part I

Besides being together for 24 years and wanting to get married, we actually *had* to get married or I would not have health insurance or diplomatic status recognized by the Dominican Republic or the State Department. Jason Vasallo, an accomplished graphic designer who once worked with Wally, designed our wedding invitation, which we e-mailed out immediately. I am indebted to Douglas and Elizabeth Smith, who were able to locate a judge in DC who was willing to marry us on short notice—and not just any judge, but Judge David Tatel of the United States Court of Appeals for the District of Columbia Circuit. Washington, DC, at the time was one of the few places in the United States where a same-sex couple could legally marry and obtain a marriage license. Judge Tatel was an approved member of the bench allowed to legally marry us. We went on November 21, 2013, to Judge Tatel's office with our witness Bonnie Berry, who is a saint and was involved in countless logistics for us. Bonnie was the person who initially took Wally through the Capital building many years earlier, introducing him to virtually every elected official in the place.

Judge Tatel's chambers were lovely, and his wife Edith was present as well. Judge Tatel has been legally blind since 1972 due to a genetic disorder, and Edith works as his set of eyes. We had some amazing personal time with him as he wanted to hear our story and get to know us a bit before he performed the ceremony. Judge Tatel had replaced Supreme Court Justice Ruth Bader Ginsburg on the DC Circuit Court and had a wonderful relationship with her. He told us he had never married a same-sex couple before, and we hold this as an revered honor. Judge Tatel wasn't exactly sure what to say when he pronounced us a legally married couple, so he called Justice Ginsburg for advice. Her advice to him was simple: you simply pronounce them "married." So here was another historic milestone for us—being married by a notable member of the judiciary, who had never married a same-sex couple, and who sought advice from a sitting Supreme Court Justice.

Following our legal wedding, we held a reception for our guests at Art and Soul, a restaurant concept by the famous chef Art Smith, who was once Oprah Winfrey's personal chef. Art is a dear friend and insisted we invite all our out-of-towners to his restaurant for the evening.

It was a spectacular night. The wedding arrangements came together extremely well but only because of the efforts of our two close friends, Steve Kemble and Dennis Centorbi. Dennis is a professional in the hospitality service industry and was able to secure the rooftop at the historic Hay Adams Hotel across the street from the White House for our wedding, along with rooms for all our guests. The weekend before Thanksgiving is a slow time in DC, but nonetheless trying to find an event space and rooms for 175 guests is not a simple process. Somehow Dennis performed a miracle. Steve is a world-renowned event planner, not a wedding planner. He coordinates and organizes huge events such as presidential inaugurations. Steve has been a close friend and worked with Wally's former company coordinating their annual conventions. He had contacts all over the world and planned our entire wedding in a few hours.

Wally's Ceremonial Swearing-In

The next day, we all gathered at the Indian Treaty Room, and Vice President Biden conducted Wally's ceremonial swearing-in ceremony. It was incredibly special as our family and friends met with the vice president in private quarters before we went through a connecting door to the Indian Treaty Room where all of our friends were waiting for the ceremony to begin. It was beyond words. I held a 104-year-old bible, provided by Wally's close and dear friend Carletta Kyles, as he placed his hand on it and repeated the words of the vice president.

OATH OF OFFICE

I, James Walter Brewster, Jr.

Do Solemnly Swear

That I Will Support and Defend

The Constitution of the United States

Against All Enemies Foreign and Domestic

That I Will Bear True Faith

And Allegiance to the Same

That I Take This Obligation Freely

Without Any Mental Reservation

Or Purpose of Evasion

And That I Will Well and Faithfully

Discharge the Duties of the Office

On Which I Am About to Enter

So Help Me God

Our Wedding, Part II

Immediately following the swearing-in, the entire group proceeded across Lafayette Park to the Hay Adams for the wedding. We all gathered on the rooftop event space where, much to my surprise, our simple wedding had grown to a full-on amazing event. Thank you, Steve! Apparently, Steve had convinced Wally without my knowledge that we needed a band, a cake, a photographer, and a full meal. The simple wedding I had envisioned had gone from a few friends to an all-out bash. It was gorgeous! The weather was incredible, much like the night of President Obama's election in 2008. We were able to open all the terrace doors, and everyone was taking pictures overlooking the White House, as it was beautifully lit in the night sky. Magical, it was all truly magical.

Joan Maloney, a real estate attorney in Chicago and dear personal friend, came to DC and conducted the most beautiful ceremony for us at the Hay Adams. It was my wedding, so of course I loved it, but it was gracious, elegant, and everything I ever thought my wedding could be—that is if the law ever allowed me to get married.

When it was time to have the ceremony, there was no walking down an aisle or any pomp and circumstance. We simply gathered in a circle with our friends surrounding us. Carletta led us in prayer and we committed our lives to each other as Joan led us in exchanging our rings. Nan and Karen provided a Unity Candle, and our family members shared hopes of light with us in a candle lighting ceremony. Then we lifted our glasses of champagne and had a heck of a party!

Part II

6: Life in the Chief of Mission Residence

Getting Settled in Santo Domingo

Now that our dream had come true, we hit the road running. Once we landed at Las Americas airport in Santo Domingo after an excruciating flight, all appeared to be smooth sailing. As we exited the jet bridge, there were security personnel and people from the U.S. embassy waiting for us. They escorted us to a small private lounge we would come to know as the ambassador's lounge. An employee from the airline took Clinton and Carter, our two West Highland White Terriers, to be inspected by a veterinarian to ensure all their paperwork and vaccinations were in order. I wasn't comfortable with this because no one informed us that our dogs would be taken away from us, but I was assured they would be well taken care of.

The Deputy Chief of Mission (DCM) Dan Foote and his lovely wife Claudia met us along with other members of the embassy staff and protocol teams. We began shaking hands with everyone. I don't have any pictures of our arrival at the airport because we were completely overwhelmed with introductions and questions about everything imaginable. Finally, Wally was told that the press had been waiting for us to arrive and was asked if he could give them a few words of introduction before we departed. Wally grabbed my hand and we walked out to the press pool.

The staff and protocol teams all walked with us out of the ambassador's lounge to meet the press. Wally gave a brief address to the press—a lot of press! I felt like I was on display like an animal in a zoo. You would have suspected these people had never seen a gay person before, and in hindsight, I could surmise maybe they hadn't. In the Dominican Republic, it was rare to openly admit to the public if you were gay.

Shortly after our arrival in-country, Cardinal Rodríguez wasted no time in making life as difficult as possible for my husband. There really wasn't much I could do to engage in the situation and although almost all processes that involved our household were fully discussed between Wally and me, this was one scenario where he had a very firm opinion: under no circumstances were we to ever address the cardinal in the press or respond to any of his vulgar statements. Trust me, I am one to defend myself and sometimes in a very public way, but my husband was right in this situation. Responding to the cardinal would only validate his warped opinion. He was incredibly powerful and had influence over a huge section of society who would never meet us, so we had to maintain an image of diplomacy and protocol.

When you are a public figure, perception is often reality in that people, including family and friends, believe what they read about you regardless of the source. Although the Dominican Republic was a small country it was still a population of 10 million, 90 percent of whom were influenced by the cardinal. Wally and I agreed that under no circumstances was I going to speak of the cardinal to anyone, specifically the media, publicly.

There were times when the media gave me an opportunity to speak but I have no doubt they really wanted some salacious story I could be tricked into or they hoped for the slight chance I would embarrass my husband. It never worked. Despite my ability to be brutally honest at times and even less than diplomatic, I wasn't immature enough to let that happen in public. I saved my meltdowns for the private quarters of our home and that was a practice that had been well-rehearsed long before Wally became a diplomat.

But today my husband is no longer the ambassador and I am no longer concerned with the impressions of the media in the Dominican Republic, so I will tell you Cardinal Nicolás de Jesús López Rodríguez is an evil man and one of the most bigoted non-Christian souls I have ever been exposed to in my life. Truly the devil incarnate! These are harsh words and no doubt will offend some, but throughout the course of my life I discovered the harm that lack of transparency can generate. Cardinal Rodríguez wielded powerful influence over the citizens of the Dominican Republic not limited to the educational curriculum, the political system, and the judicial system; he dictated Church policy over all aspects of culture and society. He lived an excessive, lavish lifestyle and according to rumor maintained intimate relationships with women. I had always heard rumors about him fathering children; recently media reports are beginning to surface in the Dominican Republic about his adulterous relationships. I don't know if these rumors are true but this much I do know: Cardinal Rodríguez never had a kind word to say for the poor or people of color, specifically those of Haitian decent. His social circles were rooted in exclusive cocktail parties and relationships with the government. He protected pedophiles and denied those who were assaulted by leaders in his Church any judicial accountability in the Dominican Republic.

My words may be offensive, but they don't come close to equaling the offensive actions the cardinal took to protect his inner circle throughout his career. I never met him personally and the ambassador and I were never put into a social environment or public event where he was, which means the cardinal also never met my husband, but clearly formed personal opinions about us.

My First Tour of Santo Domingo, 1988

It was late in the evening as we were making our final approach for landing into Santo Domingo's Las Americas International airport. I peered out the window looking for signs of life. It was pitch black but far off in the distance I could see a few lights sprinkled throughout the landscape. We were coming in over the water on our arrival and just before touchdown instantly the runway lights appeared below us.

I didn't have any preconceived ideas about what to expect. This was my first time to the Dominican Republic. I had been working for American Airlines for about a year. I was staying in the city for 36 hours. Some of the crew had been here before and mentioned the hotel was very nice with a great pool, tennis courts, and a casino.

The exit from the customs and immigration hall at Las Americas is unlike any place I had ever been. You make your way through a long hallway and past a few rental car counters. Then as you come to the exit through the automatic doors, you find yourself on a long runway with hundreds of people on either side. It was not uncommon in 1988 for practically every member of your family to greet you at the airport on your arrival. Even if you were not being greeted by anyone, it was still a great feeling because you felt the entire country was there just to welcome you.

The crew gathered outside of customs and left the airport in an old school bus that did not have any air conditioning and clearly had seen better days. As we exited the airport and headed into Santo Domingo, it was tradition to make a quick stop at a small *colmado* called Wanda's. Wanda's had the coldest beer, Presidente Grande, that everyone would buy for the long, warm ride to the hotel. After our stop at Wanda's, we made our way along the waterfront in some of the most chaotic and extreme traffic I had ever seen. Now I understood the need for something cold to drink. This clearly was going to take a while.

Since my first visit to the Dominican Republic as a crew member for American Airlines there were many different reasons that continued to draw me back to this beautiful country. The Dominican Republic has many diverse and beautiful parts including its culture, topography, and its people. I found Santo Domingo to be a wonderful city to visit; the *malecon* was vibrant and filled with nightlife, as was the Zona Colonial. It was not for the faint of heart because Santo Domingo was not really suited for tourists then. I could blend in pretty well because I have a similar skin tone and dark hair; as long as I kept my mouth shut I could move about relatively unnoticed. But the moment I attempted to speak Spanish everyone would know I was not a local.

Over the course of my many visits and my opportunity to live there, I was able to discover how fascinating the Dominican Republic is. I have had the chance to travel a large part of the world and visited many beach resorts and none compare to the Dominican Republic with its warm, crystal clear water and white sandy beaches. However, the Dominican Republic is so much more than beaches; it's sad that most people miss so much the country has to offer.

Adjusting to Diplomatic Life, 2014

Moving into a Chief of Mission Residence (CMR)—or as commonly known to non-diplomats, the ambassador's residence—is actually a pretty smooth process. The embassy team who met us at the airport escorted us in an armored SUV to our new home. As we left the airport, I was expecting it to be different than the many times I had left that airport before. This time I was in an armored SUV, but other than that, it was the same as all my previous visits. The same free-standing dilapidated pedestals lined each side of the road with the names and flags of many Caribbean nations. The road leads you to a large ramp that curves up steeply to the left and descends onto the highway that leads along the Caribbean Sea into Santo Domingo. The weather was the same typical Dominican Republic perfect: a beautiful blue sky with white puffy clouds dotting the horizon. The crystal clear water with the sun's reflection was the same, too, and we sped past, preceded by two police motorcycles and followed by the remainder of the security detail and more embassy staff. I suppose I thought the landscape would appear different because this time, it felt different for me to be there. In reality it would be. I would never be allowed to see the Santo Domingo I knew for the next three and half years—but the physical landscape was the same beautiful place I had visited so many times before.

On our arrival at the CMR, we were met by our current house staff and given a tour of the property by the post's management officer David Elmo while our bags were delivered to our master bedroom. It is all sort of like arriving at a five-star resort. We were overwhelmed at every turn and before we knew it, it was time to call it a night from what was very clearly an exhausting day.

We rounded up Clinton and Carter, and proceeded upstairs to the private quarters of the residence. We realized that we were alone for the first time that day. And there we were, the U.S. ambassador to the Dominican Republic and his husband. We had no idea what the future was about to unveil, but nonetheless we had made it. We had accomplished our goal and we were about to close our eyes for our first night in the CMR. It was a world away from my first visit to the Dominican Republic more than 25 years before, but I'd always been drawn to this place. Living here now was a dream come true.

I was pretty much confined to the house those first few days because my personal vehicle had not yet arrived. Santo Domingo is not a place you can go out on the corner and wave down a taxi so unless I was going somewhere with my husband, I was staying put. I'd heard Elton John would be playing a concert in Casa de Campo a few months later and tickets were going on sale. In Santo Domingo, you had to physically go to a ticket office to purchase a concert ticket. I was in the ambassador's office and mentioned the concert to Diane, his executive assistant—known as an OMS in the State Department—and she was also interested in going. We spread the word and got a small group together who wanted to attend the concert with us. Diane had been living there a while and had her own transportation, and she offered to take me to get tickets for everyone. Diane is a very nice career diplomat and extended her hand many times during our transition.

We drove the following morning to the ticket venue and bought the tickets, and along the way home she was kind to stop to let me run some errands since I still didn't have my car. When we returned, the gate to the CMR was broken and the security guard asked us to enter at the main gate to the embassy. Both the embassy and the CMR were on the same property but had separate entrance gates. We drove a few hundred feet down the street to the embassy entrance.

The guards knew Diane and her car, but they had never seen me before. As we pulled up they opened the exterior gate and we pulled in a few feet up to the bomb barrier and the main gate closed behind us, solidly blocking us in. The guard inspected the car and took our identification. He wanted to see my employee ID and I didn't have one. I was not an employee, I was the ambassador's spouse. Instead, I had my Diplomatic Passport issued by the U.S. State Department and my Diplomatic Cedula issued by the Dominican Republic Foreign Ministry. Diane informed the guard that I was the ambassador's husband.

Ambassador's husband? The guard had a very confused look on his face; he clearly didn't understand. How could the ambassador have a husband? It was obvious this explanation of who I was did not register with him. I seriously doubt he paid much attention to the social circles that gay people would be seen in and may never heard of or actually seen a gay person. So instead of letting us enter, he opened the gate and had Diane back out of the property. He then told me to exit the vehicle, took my IDs and phone, and left me on the street.

Diane kept telling him this was not a good idea, but she had no influence over security so she re-entered the property and went inside to straighten things out. So there I was, standing on the street locked out of my new home, without a phone or ID! Obviously I finally got back in. Someone explained to all embassy security that the new ambassador was married to a man, but to be sure this little hiccup didn't happen again, a photograph of me was distributed to every embassy security guard to avoid any future confusion. I can look back on this situation now and laugh at myself being stuck outside my new home, but at the time I was less than amused.

Exploring the Zona Colonial

The Dominican Republic was discovered by Christopher Columbus in the late 1400s and still maintains an abundance of its historical architecture in the original Zona Colonial. Santo Domingo, the first city in the Western Hemisphere, boasts so much world history, it should not be missed. Calle Las Damas, the first street, should be a requirement for any visitor. Located on the original waterfront in the old city, Calle Las Damas is home to Fortaleza Ozama, named for the Ozama river that divides east and west Santo Domingo. Many important historical buildings as well as homes of famous explorers who made Santo Domingo an important crossroads in the new world are on this stretch. The original government palace is located here, as well as the home that was built for Christopher Columbus, Colon Palace.

Santo Domingo, sadly, is not attractive to tourists. The Dominican government doesn't promote it as a tourist destination and many places within the Zona Colonial only cater to native Spanish speakers. Santo Domingo is not a place where you can stroll the streets or use public transportation with ease, and in most cases, I hate to say it, it just isn't safe. But with the appropriate precautions and a guide, anyone can navigate and enjoy it.

Zona Colonial, however, does have English/French and German speaking guides, but it will require an effort on your part to find one. The tourist train in Zona Colonial is a great option for architectural lovers but it doesn't really provide you with much history. The Zona Colonial is filled with luxury hotels, rooftop bars, nightclubs, excellent restaurants, and homes to many full-time residents.

During our tenure, I made sure every visitor who came to see us toured the Zona Colonial. After the first year, I began to use a local guide I had accidentally found while wandering through the Fortaleza Ozama. I was thrilled to find Jose, who spoke perfect English and made his full-time living as a tour guide.

Once when a small group of friends visited, we went to the Zona Colonial for lunch at one of our favorite restaurants, Pate e Palo. Wally joined us for lunch and afterward we decided to take our guests on the local tourist train around the old town. Wally coordinated with his security team that we were going to take our friends on the train—

after all cultural enlightenment and exchange is a significant part of foreign policy.

But the whole thing got completely out of hand. Instead of telling us they had security concerns, the security team approached the train operator and the head of the *cestur*, the tourist police, and basically shut down the streets while we took the train around the old city with our friends. Wally was mortified because he never in a million years would have gone on the train had he known they were going to shut down the streets of the old city. I had been on the train several times with friends, but then I am not the ambassador and the State Department does not provide security for spouses and children. On the other hand, our friends loved every minute of it and felt like celebrities because almost everyone waved and took pictures of Wally.

Preserving the Dominican Republic National Treasures

The Zona Colonial isn't the only part of the Dominican Republic a tourist should make an effort to see. The Dominican Republic is a very diverse landscape and during our time there, we made a concerted effort to visit as much of the country as possible. It isn't a small country; it is an island that shares its border with Haiti, and is the largest land mass in the Caribbean with the tallest mountain range east of the Mississippi River in North America. Pico Duarte is situated in the western Dominican Republic. It exceeds 10,000 feet above sea level and even snow flurries have been recorded at its peak. The ascent takes two days to the top and one day to descend. I always said I would climb it, but only made it to the camp entry where you meet your guides and organize your trip up the mountain. However, the drive up to the town of Jarabacoa where the excursions begin to the top of Pico Duarte is breathtaking. But it's the drive down the mountain that is truly amazing with its majestic views.

Another unique place we visited is the highest city in the Dominican Republic, Constanza. It is nestled in the mountain valley among lots of agriculture and natural forest that has been preserved by the country. It is indescribably beautiful and the temperature is absolutely perfect—no need for air-conditioning there. The lodge where we stayed had screens, so we could open the windows at night to stay cool. Wally's lead bodyguard Nelson Ramirez was from Constanza and it was a trip we always wanted to make but finding the appropriate timing was challenging taking into the consideration the distance from Santo Domingo.

Shortly after Dominican President Danilo Medina was elected for a second term, our good friend Dominguez Brito, the former attorney general of the Dominican Republic, became the minister of the environment. Most of the land surrounding Constanza is public land designated as a natural forest preserve. It is perfect for growing all types of agricultural products and as a result there is a lot of poaching of public land for private agricultural use, obviously a huge legal violation. At the time I was working with a young man named Jake Kheel, who had filmed a documentary about environmental degradation in the Dominican Republic, so this was something I found to be quite disconcerting. Wally had a conversation with Minister Brito about this potential environmental violation, because President Obama had recently signed the Paris Agreement and we were taking active measures to assist in the protection of the Caribbean's environment. After our friend Dominguez became the minister of the environment, we visited our Peace Corps volunteers in Constanza to see the progress they were making within the community.

We drove to the top of the mountain where there is a small camp and a place where one of several rivers originates. It is fascinating to see how water will slowly seep up from the natural spring deep in the earth and then within a few hundred yards form into a flowing stream of water so clean it is perfect for drinking right out of the stream. Eventually the stream becomes a river and as it moves down the mountain provides water sources for many communities along the way.

Unfortunately, this particular stream doesn't make it very far before it becomes so polluted that it is unfit for human consumption. This is because of the land poachers. These farms have been in existence for years and some of them are hundreds of acres. Their farming techniques are rather rudimentary and combined with the sewer water generated from the families living on the land and the chemicals used for farming, the water and ecosystem are quickly destroyed.

Minister Brito addressed this immediately after assuming his new position in the government over a lot of objection from the farmers.

Most Dominicans are unaware of how adversely they are being affected by these illegal farmers who continue to make a personal profit from public land.

In the Dominican Republic, the only potable water in cities and remote areas alike is from a plastic bottle that one has to purchase. If not for the land poachers, citizens could possibly have free water to drink all over the island. Our visit provided the support the minister needed to continue his quest to clear the land of these illegal poachers and hopefully he will continue his efforts for many years to come.

Potable water isn't the only environmental component in jeopardy in the Dominican Republic. Very few people know that the country is third on the list of the world's countries most affected by global warming. More than 80 percent of the country's natural reefs have disappeared due to the warming waters. As a result, the U.S. government supports a program to help NGOs rebuild the coral reef, and most of these projects are conducted with resources provided through private grants. And because 250,000 Americans live in the Dominican Republic and 1.7 million Americans visit the island every year, it is in our best interest to assist in the protection of their coral reefs.

We visited the reef restoration project and Jake took us diving down to see the actual project in action. It looked to me like trying to block Niagara Falls with sand bags but at least there precautions being taken to protect this beautiful environment.

The "Coming Out" Dinner

We arrived on November 26, 2013, two days before Thanksgiving, and Wally presented his credentials to President Medina of the Dominican Republic on December 9, 2013. I was not invited or allowed to be present for the presentation of credentials—imagine 1950 where spouses, most often women, were expected to be at home, not in public. I, however, was asked to help coordinate an introduction dinner for the new ambassador, a sort of coming out—no pun intended—to the society and business community of the Dominican Republic.

The introduction dinner turned into quite an event, and Grissette Vasquez, the protocol chief at the U.S. embassy and my eventual dear friend, worked with me hand in hand to ensure our dinner would be memorable. Virtually every member of Dominican society and leaders in the business and political community were invited to attend. As a matter of protocol, the president and first lady of the Dominican Republic along with several other palace staff were invited. Grissette informed me that although the president and first lady were invited, it was extremely unlikely they would attend, for this would set a precedent for them to attend all diplomatic events and clearly that would be impossible.

But surprise! The *primera dama* (Spanish for first lady) of the Dominican Republic Cándida Medina accepted our invitation and we couldn't have been more excited! When Grissette was informed that the *primera dama* had accepted our invitation, everything had to be reconsidered: seating arrangements, arrival logistics, who would be speaking, and so forth.

There are a lot of "opinions" about protocol and what I learned very early on is protocol professionals don't like change. In fact, they will do everything possible to not introduce a new procedure. The original seating arrangements were that I was to be seated on the dais with the ambassador, the foreign minister, and the papal nuncio. But when the *primera dama's* office accepted the invitation to attend, certain people interpreted the protocol to mean it would be inappropriate for me to be seated with the *primera dama*. I wouldn't have objected to this except for the fact I wasn't permitted to attend my husband's presentation of credentials at the palace—although I later found out it wasn't personal, it sure felt that way at the time. But being removed from the dais was something unacceptable to me. After all, this was a dinner I was co-hosting at our home with my husband.

This was a press event and every newspaper, online media, radio, and television representatives would be there. I spoke with Grissette and realized that it was the palace protocol who was controlling who would be seated on the dais with the *primera dama*, not our protocol team. It was times like this that I made Grissette's life very difficult and although I regretted putting her through so much, under no circumstances would I be standing in the audience in my own home watching my husband being introduced. It was only appropriate that I be on stage and introduce my husband because there was already an established precedent. We had attended many political and diplomatic events over the years and spouses were almost always seated at the side of their appointed or elected better halves. There were many times when we were in Vice President Biden's home and his wife Dr. Jill Biden always addressed her guests and introduced her husband. Even though the CMR was part of the embassy, it was also our home during our tenure. Palace protocol might run things in their world, but they were not going to dictate to me how things were going to run in my house.

I put so much stress on Grissette during our time in the Dominican Republic, but I am hopeful over time she realized that the archaic ways of doing business in diplomatic circles were not going to work with us. I would not be invisible, and more importantly, my husband didn't want me to be invisible. I am not sure if Grissette even informed the palace protocol office, but that evening I sat on the dais with my husband and was introduced along with the other dignitaries. Following my introduction by our DCM Dan Foote, I proceeded to the podium and introduced my husband officially for the first time to the private sector as the United States ambassador to the Dominican Republic. Dan acted as master of ceremonies and the ambassador, the *primera dama*, the acting Dominican Republic Foreign Minister Jose Manuel Trullols, and the Papal Nuncio Judes Thaddeus Okolo were all seated on the stage. The ambassador gave a few words of introduction then led a champagne toast. A flurry of camera flashes exploded from the media. I felt as if I were on the red carpet at the Oscars!

Looking back on that night, it was actually quite historic. Here we were, a legally married same-sex couple representing President Obama and the American people to a government of a foreign country where there is no separation of church and state, standing on a stage with the first lady of the host country and the Vatican's senior foreign diplomat.

The media were insane and sent a clear and powerful message to all the haters who made it their mission to discredit my husband: the president and first lady of the Dominican Republic had formally and publicly extended their hand in friendship. Immediately following the introductions and toast, we were escorted to the tented dining area for the dinner and evening's festivities.

I'll add that this event was not funded by U.S. tax dollars. In fact, Congress allocates little money for hosting dignitaries and there are strict procedures for using that money. In countries that require numerous social functions, the sitting ambassadors pay out of pocket for these events or they won't happen. The budget for the welcome dinner was almost as much as our entire budget for the year, so Wally and I wrote a check and hosted the event at our personal expense.

As we left the stage, the papal nuncio requested a brief word with the ambassador and they stepped behind the stage. When Wally arrived at the table I looked at him and his only response was, "Let's discuss it later. Just enjoy the night."

It was a beautiful January evening with bright stars twinkling over the lawn at the CMR. The tented dining areas were magnificently lit with crystal chandeliers and candlelight. It really was a perfect night—up until that one thing that went very wrong. Our management office had failed to instruct the groundskeepers to disable the automatic sprinklers that evening and during the main course, the timer engaged and water sprayed everywhere! We showered the *primera dama* and had it not been for the quick thinking of Dan Foote who threw his body over the sprinkler head, I am afraid the first lady would have experienced a full-on soaking courtesy of the U.S. embassy.

Thankfully a quick-acting staff member disengaged the sprinkler system, and the evening moved forward as planned, although I suspect Dan never fully dried out before getting home that night. As the evening concluded, we retired to our private quarters after what we felt was an extraordinarily successful first impression to Dominican society, politicians, and business leaders.

Wally told me about his conversation with the papal nuncio—and allow me to say *no bueno*! But more on that later...

The next day I arranged with Grissette to send a large bouquet of yellow tulips to the *primera dama* as an apology for the unexpected shower we gave her during our dinner. She was incredibly gracious. Fortunately that incident never adversely affected our relationship with her or President Medina.

Lies and Insults

It was customary for the Diplomatic Corps to host an annual cocktail reception for the president and first lady of the Dominican Republic every January as an expression of good will for the New Year.

All members of the Diplomatic Corps were invited and encouraged to attend with their spouses. The papal nuncio, the de-facto leader of the Diplomatic Corps, obviously was uncomfortable extending an invitation to an openly gay couple, and had secretly conducted research on my diplomatic status. I strongly suspect all of this was manipulated by the cardinal because he would obviously be attending. The Dominican Republic Foreign Ministry refused to recognize me as the legal spouse of my husband despite my being recognized as a full-fledged diplomat with all courtesies extended. They designated me as a "member of household" of the U.S. ambassador.

Deputy Assistant Secretary John Feeley of the State Department was extremely proactive in securing my diplomatic status before I arrived in-country, but the Dominican Republic Foreign Ministry—under the influence of Cardinal Rodríguez, of course—was never going to consider me an equal member of the Diplomatic Spouse Organization (Damas Diplomaticas), and it wasn't because I was a man.

Wally and I fully agreed with Deputy Assistant Secretary Feeley as to my negotiated diplomatic status, because we felt in many cases of discrimination it takes baby steps to achieve one's full goals. Would it really matter anyway? After all, who was ever going to ask for my diplomatic credentials? The papal nuncio, that' s who. I found out what he whispered to Wally the night of our party. The papal nuncio informed my husband that because I was not a fully credentialed spouse, only a credentialed member of household, that it would be impossible for him to extend an invitation for me to attend the presidential cocktail reception with my husband as a matter of protocol.

There that word was again—"protocol." It's a word I would grow to have a love/hate relationship with, mostly the latter. Barely in-country a month and we received a full-court press from the Church. The ambassador informed the papal nuncio that he would be unable to attend without me and informed the rest of the members of the Diplomatic Corps of his decision. Talk about a firestorm! We circled the wagons immediately, and Wally called the White House to converse with Valerie Jarrett, inquiring about his expected participation in the Diplomatic Corps.

Valerie informed my husband that he was asked to be the U.S. ambassador in the Dominican Republic to make his own decisions and whatever decisions those may be, he had the support of the White House. That was the last call Wally made to the White House for advice. The gauntlet was thrown, and the invitation declined.

The papal nuncio immediately issued a press announcement that the U.S. ambassador had declined to pay respects to the president and the first lady of the Dominican Republic. The announcement also declared if Mr. Satawake was to have been extended an invitation, the rest of the Diplomatic Corps was refusing to attend! This was pure fiction.

The next day the United Kingdom's ambassador to the Dominican Republic Stephen Fisher and his wife immediately issued a press release with a copy of the letter they sent to the papal nuncio, which indicated that if the spouse of the U.S. ambassador was not invited, then they would not be attending either.

The papal nuncio was caught in the media perpetuating a bold-faced lie, which I suppose is better than being caught with his pants down around his ankles on the *malecon* like the previous papal nuncio had been. The situation was eventually resolved, and the event was moved from the papal nuncio's residence to a hotel ballroom. I was extended an invitation to attend.

This was just the beginning of many exciting times ahead. Interestingly, and I am sure to the chagrin of the papal nuncio, the headlines of the newspaper that covered the event printed on the front page of their paper a huge photo of President Medina and the first lady standing alongside my husband, U.S. Ambassador James Brewster and me. I'm sure this publicity was not exactly what Papal Nuncio Judes Thaddeus Okolo was expecting.

7: Breaking Protocol

Protocol is an extraordinarily important dynamic in the world of diplomacy. It sets expectations and dictates procedures that allow for a cohesive form of communication. It also establishes traditions that can sometimes create insurmountable hurdles. Wally and I recognized the importance of protocol procedures, but we also had to consider how to balance established procedures with moving our goals forward. If boundaries were never pushed, change would never happen; it is change that allows us to grow and experience life, as well as support initiatives that improve the lives of our fellow human beings. Wally and I love to experience life, diversity, and culture that exposes us to new learning experiences. If you only ever follow the rules dictated by previous players, then how do you ever learn anything for yourself?

I love structure and predictability; after all, when there is a system of rules it's easy to meet others' expectations. But what about meeting your own expectations? How can people truly achieve their own goals playing by someone else's rules? That is how protocol can be confining. The rules that were set forth in the Dominican Republic in the diplomatic arena were based on hundreds of years of tradition. *Never* had a same-sex couple led a diplomatic mission for any member country in the Western Hemisphere. Oh, trust me, my husband was most likely not the first gay ambassador appointed to serve in the Dominican Republic—he was just the first *openly* gay ambassador and the first same-sex married gay ambassador appointed there.

On some levels, I would question why that would be a big deal, but then as it related to protocol, I can see it was a huge deal. Protocol was a very important part of our existence as diplomats, but we were entering an arena where those rigid protocols that had been cemented in centuries of tradition could not be applied to a same-sex couple. It wasn't that I wanted to disregard protocol, but there were times I had no choice.

The State Department community is overrun with protocol, so much so that it interferes with the ability for normal human communication. It also interferes with the ability to generate progress. If you work in a corporate environment, you can understand that crossing boundaries can sometimes create difficulties; however, in most cases those can be overcome. If you break protocol in the State Department, you can have a meltdown of public policy or develop an environment of jealousy and envy that results in extreme personnel discourse.

In my experience, protocol reared its head in many ways. At times, a few people made it clear I was overstepping my position, and sadly, sometimes it was those closest to me—not members of the diplomatic community as I anticipated—who expressed that sentiment. I felt like a staffer or a handler for the entire time we lived in the Dominican Republic. Staffers and handlers serve an important purpose but that wasn't my purpose. Similar to the way country folk kick an old dog when he tries to sneak into the house on a cold winter night, I was shoved away multiple times by the press because they didn't want me to appear at my husband's side on television. Wally, in his role as the ambassador, was firm on including me practically everywhere he appeared, and at times insisted I participate in meetings or official events. People often—mistakenly—assumed I was imposing myself. I knew he wanted me to be present because often he wanted to share what he was experiencing with me. Other times he simply wanted me there because he trusted my insight and judgment. Mutual trust and respect for each other's advice and insight are some of the most precious things about our relationship I cherish most. Collectively between my intuitiveness and Wally's ability to maneuver challenging situations, we have jumped a lot of hurdles together.

We have always been very open and transparent about our lives, who we are as people and what our value system is based on: inclusion. I wanted to make sure we were not bound or choked off by protocol. I wanted to respect its purpose, but I also had a purpose to further our activism and humanitarian aid efforts and would soon discover that based on the State Department protocols, it was a very unorthodox purpose.

Maneuvering the Undefined Role of a Diplomatic Spouse

Spouses are bound by expectations and restrictions that virtually handcuff us from accomplishing anything in the name of the administration we represent. Spouses are representatives of the president, but we are not recognized employees, we are not paid, we are not allowed to use the resources of the embassy without specific special permission, and we are never allowed to ride in the ambassador's vehicle without the ambassador present. That would be considered personal use and a violation of State Department rules. Spouses and children are not provided any security whatsoever. We operate a household behind bars (sometimes literal bars!) and are not provided any assistance to maneuver through the bureaucratic process that requires us to run a household full of staff that technically do not work for us but work in our house every day! A portion of the ambassador's salary is deducted monthly to pay a part of the salaries of the house staff along with other private uses of the residence. Therefore, the household staff works for the ambassador. I realize this sounds like a lot of whining but it was extremely difficult to manage—or as the Dominicans say, *muy complicado!*

Although I had attended the Ambassadorial Training Seminar as a spouse, it was really nothing more than a courtesy experience. Patrick Kennedy, who oversaw management and personnel at the State Department, ineloquently informed me spouses are not employees of the State Department. The role of an ambassador's spouse is clearly undefined, which contributes to all sorts of difficulties for the ambassador and his or her family. There are an extraordinary amount of expectations, some realistic and some not, and there is not a specified platform. Basically you are winging it with few resources to help you along the way.

For all practical purposes, ambassador's spouses are highly restricted from working in the country where they are posted, unlike the spouses of all other career diplomats who can work at the embassy. Spouses are not allowed to work at the embassy due to nepotism (something that clearly doesn't apply to our current executive branch of government). Everyone who works at the embassy ultimately reports to the ambassador, and as the spouse of the ambassador you can't report to your own spouse. Spouses of ambassadors are restricted from working for private businesses or organizations that have relationships with the U.S. embassy. They can't work for a foreign entity doing business in their host country. So basically, spouses can't work. All that is left are hosting events at the CMR and the humanitarian initiatives the embassy is working on, if allowed by the coordinator and upon the ambassador's approval. Not having the ability to work was not something that negatively affected me; what did, however, was how certain members of the embassy used that to manipulate me into agreeing to things I didn't want to do.

Vice President Joe Biden was very forthright about his support of ambassadors' spouses and the role they play in American diplomacy. Throughout his career, the vice president supported the official recognition of the role of an ambassador's spouse. As recently as March 16, 2018, at an event in Pittsburgh celebrating the life of Ambassador Dan Rooney, who served as the U.S. envoy in Ireland and owner of the Pittsburgh Steelers, the vice president reiterated to Mr. Rooney's widow that he repeatedly introduced legislation supporting that ambassadors' spouses receive salaries. This would have at minimum put some parameters in place on which one could at least attempt to meet the expectations they are arbitrarily saddled with when they enter the diplomatic arena as a spouse.

I can see both sides of the argument, there are spouses of ambassadors who want nothing to do with the expectations placed on them. I have spoken with those who had no desire to engage with the diplomatic community and there are countries where the expectations are minimal and unnecessary and no spouse should be required to participate because they are married to an ambassador. But the overwhelming majority of assignments throughout the world require the support and input of an ambassador's spouse. They are expected to support initiatives, organize, arrange, accommodate and participate in meetings. They are expected to spend their own money and provide their own transportation to embassy events where there is a significant expectation of their presence. At the very least they should be provided with an official platform in which to function in the role if they are willing.

Exit Protocols

As ambassador, Wally couldn't really do much about the media and was unable to rely on our public affairs team to handle them in those specific moments. When we first arrived in the country there were press at every event we attended. When the ambassador's motorcade arrived at a large event with press, the vehicle was always positioned where the ambassador would exit the vehicle closest to the door he was entering.

This left the ambassador's spouse or anyone accompanying him or her with the challenge of exiting the car on the opposite side and then catching up. This may sound a bit ridiculous but in reality, it presented challenging situations for me to navigate. For security reasons, the ambassador can't open the door from the inside of the vehicle; he must wait for a member of the security detail to open it from the outside so they can be in position to accompany the ambassador into the building. The press in the Dominican Republic were very aggressive; the security detail had to be in place surrounding Wally before they would open my car door or they would have to open my door and then immediately run to the other side to open the ambassador's. Either way, it usually left me following behind, pushing my way through the crowd of reporters as the security team swiftly took the ambassador into the venue.

Early in our tenure after experiencing this a few times, Wally and I had a huge argument about this process. To me, it was simple: security either opened my door first and allowed me time to get around to the other side of the car so we could enter an event together or I wasn't going. I was on the business end of so many other discriminations, indignities, and "protocols"—the Catholic Church felt I should never leave the house, invitations would arrive addressed to "Ambassador and Guest," our press team for a time would actually undermine our public persona—which all paled in comparison to this. I was done being treated like a second-class citizen when I was in public with my husband. I wasn't going to follow behind my husband into event after event like a member of the support team who stands in the corner waiting for all the photos to be taken of the principal.

Wally is not good at offending people; he is very diplomatic and if he thinks for a moment he was going to hurt someone's feelings he would maneuver the situation at all cost. He made efforts to improve the situation, but this was something that I just eventually came to terms with. It was much bigger than the ambassador. This was something that was based on decades of protocol practices and therefore, was never really truly resolved.

Establishing Trust

Shortly after we arrived, we began holding courtesy calls with various members of society, government, social organizations, and humanitarian groups. This quickly became controversial because we met with leaders of various LGBT organizations who were working for the equality of their community in the Dominican Republic.

In retrospect, these controversies were a sampling of our new life in the Dominican Republic, which began the day we arrived. The media were simply obsessed that the new ambassador for the United States was a gay man who was open and transparent and, most shockingly, married to a man with whom he would be seen in public. Stress also existed within the CMR.

Upon reflection, I now view an ambassador's arrival at an embassy similar to a deer walking into a wolf's den: no one is going to protect you, and it's just a matter of who is going to get the biggest bite! Despite some true professionals who looked out for Wally and even some who looked out for me—and it was unfavorable for them to do so because access to the ambassador is restricted based on rank—it was a difficult situation for all to navigate. It's much like in the military: those who have access sometimes are persecuted if they appear to have too much contact.

We were fortunate that there were two men who worked at the embassy who would become dear friends and confidants to both of us, despite any negative fallout they may have faced. Gary Lowman, a career foreign service officer, and Brock McCormack, his husband. Gary and Brock had been in the Dominican Republic long enough to know the lay of the land in the LGBT community as well as the particulars of the embassy community. Both communities required delicate maneuvering, and Gary and Brock offered us invaluable guidance. Gary and Brock didn't become friends and advisors because they were another gay couple in the complicated world of diplomacy; they became friends and advisors because they were two of the few people who extended their hand in friendship.

Wally and I had a lot of conversations about what his work and leadership would look like once we arrived at the CMR. We discussed the kind of leadership he would like to implement and how he would

My husband being sworn in as the U.S. Ambassador by Vice President Joe Biden. The family bible was 104 years old and belonged to our dear friend.

Overlooking the White House the night of our wedding with Moises and Austria Alou.

Our wedding with Carletta Kyles a life friend offering the blessing.

The passing of light ceremony with family and friends at our wedding just before we jointly lit the unity candle.

Off and running on our wedding day!

Me, First Lady Cándida Medina, Wally, Dominican Republic Foreign Minister Jose Manuel Trullols, and Papal Nuncio Judes Thaddeus Okolo at Wally's introduction to the Dominican Republic. This was the evening the papal nuncio informed my husband I would not be welcome at diplomatic events.

Grissette Vasquez, thank you for every moment of support and inspiration. I never would have survived without you!

Being banned from John the Baptist school!

Visiting with a group of students learning English at Bi-National Center in Santo Domingo supported by our embassy.

My dear friend Maribel cohosting the Primera Dama of the Dominican Republic at our home for International Women's Day Luncheon.

Attending the arrival ceremony of Prime Minister David Cameron of the United Kingdom and our first State Dinner with President Obama and guests.

Our dear friends and fellow diplomats Gary Lowman, a career foreign service officer, and his husband Brock McCormack joining us for one of the many diplomatic events we attended. We like to call this the new face of diplomacy!

Fourth of July at the U.S. embassy in Paris.

The countless number of times we joined Moises and Austria Alou to support our Dominican team Leones del Escogido!

The first time we welcomed the First Lady of the Dominican Republic Cándida Medina to our home along with DCM Dan Foote and his wife Claudia.

In awe of the fireworks display at our first Fourth of July celebration along with UK Ambassador Steven Fisher.

The end of our first Fourth of July celebration in the Dominican Republic. I was asking Grissette, "What are we doing next year?"

In response to the Pulse nightclub shooting in Orlando, this memoriam was displayed in our foyer at the ambassador's residence.

Just before leaving the Dominican Republic for the final time as a diplomat, my husband was invited by President Medina to the Palace for a farewell conversation. President Medina specifically asked if I would attend and I was honored to accompany my husband.

be able to execute his initiatives. There wasn't a single agenda item I recall specifically targeting. He wanted to provide support to the professionals who ran various departments and do what he could to advance their initiatives. Once his nomination was announced he received numerous congratulatory calls from personal friends in the Dominican Republic and many of them certainly had agendas they would like to have seen addressed. Some were legitimate, pertaining to government relationships, commerce, trade and so forth; and others, however, were personal matters that an ambassador does not have the ability to influence. But that doesn't stop people from asking.

No one ever brought up the "gay agenda"—and it never crossed our minds that it would be an issue we would have to address—except for Cardinal Rodríguez, of course. That man directed considerable hatred toward gay people. Once the cardinal made his vulgar public comments about my husband upon his nomination, the gay community in the Dominican Republic reacted with public cries of support, leaving us no choice but to address the issue with our community. Gary had worked closely with USAID outreach to the LGBT community of the Dominican Republic through protocol channels at the embassy and was familiar with the leaders of those organizations. With Gary's advice and leadership, he set forth our communication process in addressing the gay community's concerns and the human rights violations they experienced. Through that process Gary also became an advisor on other issues of extreme importance of the bilateral relationship between the U.S. and the Dominican Republic, specifically on navigating the intricacies of the U.S. embassy.

More importantly, Gary and Brock became my friends, thereby separating the protocol of being diplomats and just being nice, genuine human beings. It is small things that can bring you the biggest joy, and one of the biggest joys I remember was when the ambassador was traveling and I was home alone in the Dominican Republic. Gary and Brock invited me to dinner at their home. We had an amazing time eating pasta, sharing wine, and engaging in non-political, non-embassy conversation. During our conversation we learned that we all enjoyed singing karaoke. I am a horrible singer but I love singing karaoke! We ended up singing karaoke until the wee hours of the morning. No guards, no staff, just good friends having fun without the intrusion of diplomatic life.

Gary and Brock weren't the only people who befriended us. Another fond experience I remember was "sneaking out of the CMR" with my good friend Allen. I say "sneaking out" in quotes because technically I wasn't restricted to the CMR; I was free to come and go as I pleased. I didn't need permission from the guards who protected the residence—they were there to protect the property of the United States, not me. However, they did keep a record of all people who came and went, including me. Allen worked in the embassy in some capacity that wasn't entirely clear to me; I am sure it had something to do with a job that I didn't have a security clearance to know about. We had become good friends and I highly respected his commitment to the United States and his work for the American people. It was late, and he had been over for dinner.

The ambassador had an early meeting the next morning and went to bed. Allen and I continued conversing about life and I mentioned it would be nice to go out and grab a drink at the *colmado* a few blocks away. So with Allen by my side, we walked out the guard gate and to the *colmado*. We sat on green plastic chairs on the sidewalk with the rest of the locals and shared a Presidente Grande. The *colmado* was on a corner of a busy intersection where cars exited the highway onto the local street. It was full of all local patrons, who would gather at these neighborhood venues late at night to drink and share stories. This was the real-life culture of everyday Dominicans and I loved being there in the purity of their culture. The music was loud and could be heard blocks away, the bare light bulbs strung on the ceiling provided so much light that it reflected off the stop sign a block away, but also provided adequate lighting for the dominoes and card games that were being played. A few people danced between the sparse tables and the bar. It was a casual place—no designer clothes, no expensive jewelry, no luxury cars lined the streets—just everyday working-class people. We were having a great time until Allen's phone rang and embassy security had been notified by the guards at the residence that we had left on foot and disappeared into the dark night. They were concerned where I was and why I had left. As I said, security was not there to protect me, but they certainly kept tabs on me. We finished our beers and returned to the residence. I didn't "sneak out" again—I didn't need my husband receiving reports on my protocol faux pas.

Making Friends and Influencing Career Diplomats

Once we were settled in, we wanted to extend our hand of friendship to all employees of the embassy. We had never lived outside of the United States and knowing a lot about the Dominican Republic, we felt it would be nice to get to know the community working at the embassy.

We discovered early on that there are three types of employees at a U.S. embassy abroad: career State Department diplomats, members of the locally engaged staff (LES, who were Dominican citizens who work for the U.S. State Department at the embassy), and the ambassador. There are also protocols at play when interacting with employees, as we soon found out.

Shortly after arriving at our "post," a term used by State Department professionals, we met a young man who would become a good friend and big supporter. He and his wife were at our home for dinner, and we were talking about his experiences living and working abroad as a U.S. citizen. He had met his wife in Europe, and she was from Slovenia. I was fascinated with his world travels and experiences, and wanted as much information about their lives as he was willing to share. I have no doubt one day he will be serving the American people in the U.S. Congress or even the White House.

We also chatted about Wally's and my experiences and backgrounds. At some point in the conversation, the subject of "politically appointed ambassadors"—a term I had developed a loathing for—surfaced and he confirmed to me what we had been hearing all along: many State Department career professionals hold a negative view of ambassadors who come from the private sector. The impression is they are taking jobs away from career professionals who dedicate their entire lives to the U.S. government and feel that their counterparts from the private sector are not equally prepared to conduct themselves effectively in the role. The State Department professionals have a general belief that the politically appointed ambassadors merely donated a few thousand bucks to the person who became president, and in return, they are provided with this extraordinary opportunity. Let me set the record straight here, much the same as I did with my good friend that night at dinner: those who are appointed work just as hard and are just as committed to the cause as any career diplomat. The reality is all ambassadors are appointed by the president of the United States and therefore should be referred to as presidential appointees.

We felt that these protocol hurdles needed to be circumvented so in an effort to normalize relationships in the embassy and recognize the equality and contribution of all our team members, we held formal dinners at our residence twice a month for more than a year to meet and greet every single person who worked with the ambassador. We discovered that many people who worked for the U.S. embassy in Santo Domingo, in some cases for more than 20 to 30 years had *never* been invited to the ambassador's residence. I was horrified.

Yes, we paid for all these dinners with our personal resources; not a single penny of taxpayer money can be used to host events for embassy employees. That didn't matter to us. We simply wanted to give the embassy staff and community the opportunity to get to know us as people—after all they had been enduring a media storm for four months before we even arrived in-country and who knows what they believed about us. And we wanted an opportunity to get to know them as well.

In the beginning it went well, but then we discovered that some people were being invited to certain dinners and their counterparts or bosses had not yet been invited; as a result, jealousy and envy blossomed. I thought to myself, "Seriously people, this isn't high school. Everyone will eventually get a date to the prom, just calm down." In hindsight, maybe it was naïve to believe a simple extended hand of friendship would not be received as such, but for the most part people extended their hands in return. I respect most protocols and long-standing customs, but I learned that many of these customs would prevent progress along the way.

Receiving High-Profile Dignitaries

Everyone wants to feel relevant. When you are continually made to feel otherwise it can have very adverse effects on your relationships. I loved when principals from Washington visited; those were the times I was able to participate freely and actually feel needed and validated. Vice President Biden promised Wally he would come to the Dominican Republic to see us, and he kept that promise. As with any visit of that caliber, everyone wants to play a role in the operation. Except for Wally and me, the rest of the career diplomats wanted to be seen as impactful and effective. Wally and I wanted to feel that way, too, but our future with the State Department was limited, unlike our colleagues who would continue their careers for years to come. So for them the opportunity to participate in high-level visits was the opportunity to get their skills in front of decision makers.

Fortunately, Wally and I had a relationship with the vice president long before he came to visit us in the Dominican Republic. Wally insisted that I be present for every event and appearance of his time in the country. I personally previewed his accommodations at the hotel ensuring they were acceptable and walked through the space they had chosen. I was involved in site selections and organizing the invitation list for the embassy reception. The meet and greet was held at the embassy and not our residence because Vice President Biden wanted to greet every employee and their children. He is truly a genuine and caring man who loves the United States of America, and he respects our diplomatic relationships and diligently works to ensure freedom and democracy on a global scale. He also loves and cares for every member of our foreign service and the dedication and sacrifice they make serving the United States around the world. I can easily tell when politicians take the time to greet constituents and their fellow citizens with a genuine extended hand of compassion and when they are just going through the motions. I have been campaigning since I was 14 years old and I have seen it all; there is no doubt in my mind Vice President Biden would stand for days in a receiving line if that is what it took to ensure everyone who wanted to meet him had the opportunity.

In preparation for Vice President Biden's visit to the Dominican Republic, President Medina insisted I be asked to join the ambassador and the vice president at the National Palace along with our DCM Dan Foote and his wife Claudia. We obviously didn't sit in on the official diplomatic discussions, but for media purposes we were included. Along with the support staff and local embassy colleagues, we waited in a beautiful ballroom of the National Palace while the bilateral meetings were taking place. President Medina and the staff at the National Palace went to great lengths to make us feel welcome. The ballroom where we were was lined with large oversized paintings and the ceiling was extraordinarily ornate with hand-carved inlays. One entire side of the ballroom was flanked by a series of large double doors that opened onto a central interior courtyard of the palace. The ceramic tile floors inside the ballroom and outside along the corridors were museum quality. I occasionally would make an excuse to go the restroom so I could have the chance to look at the architecture of the interior courtyard and the exterior of the building. I have had the opportunity to visit palaces all over the world and this was one of the most beautiful I had ever seen. I only wish I could have toured the entire building.

The protocol team from President Medina's office kept coming to the ballroom to talk with Vice President Biden's staff and keep them informed of the progress. It was being communicated that President Medina didn't want to hold a joint press conference with Vice President Biden after the bilateral discussions. No reason was given, but they just didn't think it was a good idea.

This was very confusing for Vice President Biden's staff. I knew Vice President Biden's chief of staff Fran Person very well, and he finally came over and asked my thoughts. I explained to him that the palace protocol could be very difficult and they often blocked access to President Medina. The National Palace had a large community of LGBT people working there, although they were mostly in the closet and wouldn't openly admit they were gay, they were always very nice and appropriate to the ambassador and me, so I told Fran I would be happy to talk to the one person I knew in the protocol office. He was one of the staff members from the palace who was relaying the information.

I knew it wasn't President Medina who was balking on a press conference. It made no sense—standing next to Vice President Biden following bilateral meetings about the future of our diplomatic relationships was good press. It had to be someone else and I suspected it was the protocol chief for the palace, who did not like us at all. So I pulled out my negotiation skills from my real estate days and opened the conversation with "let me help you help the president." I explained that brief remarks in a joint press conference with the vice president would allow him to adorn President Medina with accolades that could potentially boost his popularity among Dominicans who lived in the United States. Vice President Biden was extremely popular during the Obama administration and a few kind words from him couldn't hurt. They agreed and ultimately the joint press conference happened and, exactly as I suspected, was a success. I don't take credit often for things but in this case I was instrumental in the outcome. It was also extremely validating to me that the vice president's chief of staff consulted me on my opinion. These experiences didn't happen a lot, but when they did it proved to me that I was relevant and an important part of our influence in the Dominican Republic.

Once the bilateral talks were coming to an end, Claudia Foote, the Deputy Chief of Mission's wife, and I were positioned outside the doors of the room where the talks were being held. I am not sure whose decision this was but again it was one of those rare situations where we as spouses were included. These types of scenarios are very coordinated to the point of who exits the doors first and in what order do they speak to the press, if they speak at all.

Anytime you see large events with presidents and other world leaders, there has been weeks of planning in the process to make it happen. Staff members and other support personnel spend weeks coordinating where they will stand, where they will sit, who will speak first, who they shake hands with at the beginning or the end or both, and so on. No detail, specifically if the press are going to be present, is left for chance. As we left the hallway to proceed across the interior courtyard of the National Palace to the Hall of Ambassadors where the press conference would be held, the vice president of the Dominican Republic, Margarita Cedeno de Fernandez, came over to say hello and slipped her arm into mine and guided me into the Hall of Ambassadors. If anyone is aware of what it is like to stand in the shadows, it is Vice President de Fernandez.

I had never been in the Hall of Ambassadors. It was a special place for me to visit, not because of the event that was taking place at the moment, but because it was where my husband presented his credentials to President Medina when he arrived in the Dominican Republic. That was the ceremony I was not allowed to attend.

Navigating Protocol, 2013

Wally was committed to his work in the Dominican Republic and, with rare exception, everyone who knew him and worked with him agreed he had the best interest of the bilateral relationship in mind with every decision he made. There are many different types of Ambassadors, and as we learned in the Ambassadorial seminar, there is not a blueprint for the job.

Depending on the country, there are extreme differences in priorities. The Dominican Republic, we soon learned, was a country that could benefit from a more aggressive approach on matters such as security, drug trafficking, money laundering, human trafficking, immigration fraud, corruption of various sorts, education, public health, commerce, and a multitude of humanitarian causes and many more initiatives. There is no possible way one person could focus on all of these matters and be effective at them all.

Wally focused on the day-to-day operations of the embassy and its major initiatives that required a level of security clearance I did not have, and left the social calendar and humanitarian efforts for me to sort out. Any social events that took place at the CMR and the humanitarian initiatives that were important to us were where I would spend my time and personal resources doing what I could to influence. Spouses of U.S. Ambassadors unfortunately are somewhat restricted when it comes to initiating projects, but as long as they are for the benefit of the bilateral relationship and directed by the Ambassador, then progress can be made.

Unfortunately, there were a handful of people who from day one decided to make our lives as miserable as possible. There was one particular scenario very early on where the boundary had to be defined immediately. Because there are not defined roles for an ambassador's spouse, my husband chose to use my abilities as much as possible where appropriate. There was one very clear opportunity where I could be of service to him and his embassy and that was coordinating events that took place in our home. The CMR is the private home of the ambassador, but it is to be used at every opportunity possible to promote and extend the hand of American democracy. This was the only domain where as a spouse I had the obvious opportunity to provide input and influence.

In the Dominican Republic, the U.S. embassy National Day celebrating U.S. Independence Day was the single most important event in the country next to the country's own independence celebration, *27 Febrero*. Anyone and everyone wanted an invitation to this event. My husband had priorities beyond planning parties, but the Fourth of July event was too important to leave to the embassy staff, so he directed me to be his eyes and ears in the development process. He initially directed me to meet with Grissette Vasquez, the protocol chief, and develop a theme for the event and discuss the fundraising procedures previous administrations had taken to produce the event.

The Fourth of July celebration was the only project the embassy undertook that could be funded by private sector money. It made sense: one would not want business or government in a foreign country having influence in the day-to-day operations of the U.S. embassy. However, for the Fourth of July event, we could reach out to American businesses represented in the Dominican Republic and encourage them to financially support the celebration.

Traditionally the event took place at the CMR, and although our property had beautiful gardens and plenty of space to conduct the event, I had grander ideas. I spoke with multiple career and non-career spouses around the world about their plans and execution of their Fourth of July events. After consulting with Grissette and our management officer David Elmo, I realized that moving the event to a public venue would create a multitude of security concerns and, in their minds, give us less control over the entire project. Society in the Dominican Republic expected an invitation to the ambassador's residence. I had the privilege of attending one Fourth of July event a few years earlier at the U.S. ambassador's residence in France, so at least I had a vision of the impression we wanted to leave with the Dominican people. Despite being under extreme scrutiny by the Dominican media because we were a same-sex couple, we felt pressured to perform better than any other previous diplomatic administration at the U.S. embassy in Santo Domingo. For this reason, Wally wanted my eyes and ears on the project.

After my initial meeting with Grissette and David, where we developed a theme and set a fundraising goal for the event, it was time to enact our plan. The next morning, I was home when I received a call from a member of the cultural affairs team at the embassy. He wanted an opportunity to discuss with me my ideas for the Fourth of July event and was asking if we could set up a meeting at my convenience. I was extremely flattered at first, while at the same time questioned why the embassy employees don't communicate with each other. I gladly received his invitation to discuss our goals. Later that morning our cultural affairs attaché came to the CMR to meet with me, which at the time only required him to walk about 100 yards across our backyard.

When we first arrived in the Dominican Republic, the new embassy was under construction. The embassy was still operating out of the old building, which was located in the backyard of our new home. Our conversation got off to a great start as I repeated most everything I had discussed with Grissette and David, and he confirmed the ideas were fresh and very different from anything they had done before. *But...*

I would soon learn there was always a "but" in bureaucracy. After he indulged me for about 30 minutes, he proceeded to tell me that the Fourth of July celebration was actually an event conducted under the direction of the cultural affairs division of the embassy, and because he was the cultural affairs attaché, he appreciated my input and would take my suggestions into consideration as they moved forward.

I had obviously made a serious faux pas and had no idea this was the case. I had assumed since the ambassador had instructed Grissette and David to include me in all decisions regarding the celebration that it was understood I would be participating in the decisions and take the lead role in coordinating the event. I immediately apologized for my overstep and assured him I in no way meant to exceed my authority and appreciated him explaining to me the procedures that were in place. He was very kind and thanked me for my understanding.

I did, however, have a question of our cultural affairs attaché: Where would he be holding the Fourth of July event? This question confused him as he looked at me and responded simply, "Here." I then asked my second question. "Where is here?" He must have thought I was a complete idiot as he sat up in his chair and responded, "Here at the CMR." I then looked at him and said, "The CMR? You mean my home?" "Yes, the CMR," he responded.

The embassy personnel loved using the term "CMR" as a method of depersonalizing the ambassador's residence, which in reality was the ambassador's and his family's home. Although the ambassador's home was used on occasion for positively impacting certain events, it was still his home and he and his family did have a say as to what took place there. After all, a portion of an ambassador's salary each month is allocated to subsidize the private use of the residence, unlike every other State Department employee who is provided with housing without making any contribution to the monthly cost. Additionally, if the U.S. Embassy employees have school-aged children, the U.S. government pays the full cost of the children's private school education at the very best schools available in that host country.

So, when I was told my ideas would be "taken into consideration" and my further input—which in actuality was the ambassador's input and the implementation of which I was responsible for ensuring would be considered—I was naturally taken aback. After a deep breath I calmly informed him that any event, reception, dinner, or even the mowing of the lawn that took place at my home would be under the ambassador's and my supervision. If this was not acceptable to him and his cultural affairs team, then he was most welcome to find an acceptable location of his choice to hold his celebration. I wasn't trying to be indignant, but it was clear that this embassy employee would do anything to make things as difficult as possible. In this case I asserted my rightful influence.

He agreed with my position and I remained on the team to coordinate the event, but I will say he craftily took every opportunity to make things as difficult as possible. I later discovered he was the spouse of a career diplomat, so in reality he could never be fired because his job was somewhat of a courtesy position and he used that to make my life difficult. However, he highly underestimated my tenacity for difficult situations, and we moved forward with our plans to hold the party at the ambassador's and my home, and executed what would be known as one of the most notable U.S. embassy Fourth of July celebrations in the history of the Dominican Republic. And we repeated that for the next two years!

The only other slight hurdle I had to address was the guest list. The procedure of compiling the guest list would be for each division within the embassy to generate their own list and then send it to the protocol office. Protocol was more inclined to ensure the "right" people were invited. The embassy staff is not insular in the respect they may work in the embassy, but they live and socialize locally. Sometimes there are bad people who intentionally attempt to infiltrate the embassy through developing friendships with embassy employees. Although I understood this position, I was more concerned with inclusiveness, which was something that was lost on Dominicans. Grissette procured each department's list and then, once consolidated, security reviewed the list for any potential risks.

I, too, wanted to ensure that the ambassador's and my guests were included, so I developed my own list and submitted it for review. Grissette called me one afternoon and asked to meet. By this time, I knew if Grissette wanted to meet face-to-face it was because she was disturbed by something. She always came to the residence so we could speak privately, because anytime I would go to the embassy, it was public knowledge. Now, I adore Grissette as much as life itself, and every time she raised an issue with me it was from a place of genuine and sincere concern. I never doubted her dedication and commitment to the ambassador and his well-being. Grissette was a consummate professional, but sometimes protocol got in her way.

When I submitted my guest list to her office, it included personal friends from Chicago, family, our inner circle from the Dominican Republic, and various others. One group I included were the leaders of the LGBT community in Santo Domingo and Santiago. This raised an eyebrow. Keep in mind that these were activists, and activism was a dirty word in the Dominican Republic at this time. But the bigger concern was that these people were *gay*! I didn't see this as a problem; after all, the ambassador and myself are gay. But apparently in the eyes of the "right" people, we were different than regular gay people. One of my dearest and closest confidants said that to me early on when we arrived in the Dominican Republic and frankly, I was offended.

There is not a "different type of gay." There is only one type of gay, and that's gay! Every human being has unique features and beauty, some have more money, some are more educated, some are born with blue eyes, and some like me are born with brown skin, but the one thing we all are is human. So the idea that others were concerned that I was inviting gay people to my home perplexed me. It was explained to me that the "right" people could be offended if the gay people showed up and were photographed or if society discovered they were at an event with gay people. I literally laughed out loud and simply informed Grissette that if the "right" people were offended by the guests we invited to our home, then they could just leave through the same door they entered. I would not be dictated by the concerns of people whom I had never even met. Let's just say the "gays" came to the party and no one left.

Texas in the Dominican Republic

Fourth of July events are a direct reflection of the U.S. embassy community and the U.S. ambassador. Wally is extremely sensitive to image and branding, after all he is an expert in the field and understands all too well that perception is in many cases reality. We could not fail, we would not fail; everything we did in the Dominican Republic was watched by the press, media, and influencers like a virus under a microscope. We were 100 percent committed to success, and that would be measured by the impression we would leave on the Dominican people and how that reflected on President Obama and his administration. We would not allow the haters to win.

The first Fourth of July event we oversaw in the Dominican Republic would be extraordinary by any measure. The theme was Texas BBQ! Wally is a Texan through and through. Although we lived in Chicago longer as adults than we had lived in Texas, it was his home. A quick warning to those of you who marry Texans: you might move away, but someday you will be drawn back.

A Texas barbecue sounds simple, and it certainly can be, but in our eyes it was necessary to raise the bar to a new level. We implemented a few elements to add a bit of flair and elegance to the evening—this would be no paper-plate-and-Styrofoam-cup event. David assembled an exceptional team to coordinate the celebration, and except for a couple of naysayers, we became a motivated and excited group of people working on the project.

To Grissette's chagrin, I implemented a suggested dress code of white shirts and jeans. Dominicans are extraordinarily glamorous people, and the private sector is amazingly fashionable—after all it is the home of Oscar de la Renta! Grissette felt suggesting something as casual as jeans and white shirts would make the event seem less glamorous. When someone suggested we hand out cowboy hats at the entrance, she nearly passed out. But we did hand out cowboy hats—500 to be exact—in the receiving line as our guests entered the party.

Britten Tillinghast and the Shakedown Authority performed live country music, barbecue sizzled on the grill, and our dear friend and world famous chef Art Smith, former personal chef of Oprah Winfrey, prepared 1,000 pieces of fried chicken and baked 500 cupcakes with American flags in each one. Food was served on china plates and drinks were mixed in real cocktail glasses. Summer in the Caribbean usually forecasts rain, so the backyard sported three tented pavilions, complete with candlelight and chandeliers. And finally, we had constructed a covered entry hall with air conditioning in the event anyone overheated and needed a place to cool down. It was truly magical and despite a few hiccups that I can't even remember, we received more than 1,600 guests to what will be remembered as one of the most impactful celebrations ever conducted by our diplomatic mission.

The evening ended with a fireworks display that would swell the heart and pride of any American. And it all went off perfectly without a drop of rain! What began as something that to the embassy team was completely unorthodox turned out to be exciting and motivating for everyone involved. As the evening came to a close I gave Grissette a big hug and thanked her for being my rock through the months of planning and wiping sweat from our brow. I looked her straight in the eye and asked, "So what are we going to do next year to top this?" I think she wanted to shoot me.

Finding Support

Protocol being what it is, it isn't always a bad thing. For the most part, the staff at the CMR was beyond competent, and with a few exceptions, worked together to keep the inner workings of the house running smoothly, especially on the fly when VIPs were in town.

We had just returned from the Memorial Day holiday in early June 2016 and jumped directly into preparations for the Organization of American States (OAS) General Assembly meetings to be held in Santo Domingo June 13–15. In addition to the many foreign dignitaries who would be arriving in the Dominican Republic, the U.S. delegation would also be coming from Washington, DC, and this would require virtually the entire embassy staff to prepare for all the movements that would take place with each principal participating, including the Secretary of State John Kerry. It was another all-hands-on-deck situation.

The embassy staff was extraordinary in these situations, everyone wanted an opportunity to be recognized by visiting dignitaries, after all these were colleagues that could make or break their careers. The week proved to be rather intense, in addition to the regular schedule of events including a Youth Cultural Festival, organized by Melba Grullon, who had become a strong ally and supporter of the ambassador, practically every hour of every day would impact the ambassador's schedule allowing very little time for sleep. To ensure the residence and staff were prepared for the dignitaries' visits and last minute off-schedule meetings that would take place at our home, we also were preparing for a debrief dinner at the residence following the wrap up of the OAS meetings with senior staff from Washington. A dinner I might add that had no confirmed guest list.

CMR events were typically very structured, but due to the schedule of the OAS meetings, we had no idea which State Department personnel would decide to come to dinner. Although it was a little stressful, I must say we had the most outstanding and professional residence staff in the world. I often exchanged messages with fellow spouses about how wonderful the residence staff was and that they could respond to any situation without hesitation or controversy.

Toward the end of our tenure in the Dominican Republic I finally felt respected. Not because of any one specific thing, but more so that people just treated me as a normal person. They got used to seeing me in the grocery store, a local *colmado,* or at a café around town. I loved it when I could get a reservation at a restaurant without being required to ask someone to call and use the ambassador's name to get me a table. I was able to communicate on my own and not need influence, just a simple text message was all it took. I know it may sound silly, but living in an environment where you have to rely on everyone around you to do things for you, not having freedom to come and go from your own house without being searched like an outsider, or needing to call your husband's secretary or bodyguard to reach him is just not normal. It was very emasculating and there was little resolution to the situation. Some protocols you just can't break no matter how hard you try.

8: Cardinal Sins

The Papal Nuncio Scandal

By the time we had begun to settle into our post in the Dominican Republic in early 2013, our old nemesis Cardinal Rodríguez was still campaigning hate against us.

What is most interesting about the cardinal's villainous attempts to discredit my husband was that the cardinal was in the midst of an enormous scandal within the Church. I suspect he used my husband's nomination as a diversion.

While Wally and I were preparing for our transition to the Dominican Republic, there was an investigation around the personal activities of the Archbishop Joseph Wesolowski, the papal nuncio in the Dominican Republic. Nuria Piera, a senior reporter and director for CDN Television in Santo Domingo, had been investigating rumors that Wesolowski allegedly was molesting young homeless boys in the Zona Colonial.

According to reports by Piera and her investigative team, the papal nuncio would often venture off alone to the *malecon* late at night. The *malecon* is a section of waterfront along Santo Domingo's coastline that is littered with small bars, restaurants, casinos, touristy hotels, as well as gentlemen's clubs and houses of ill repute. The reports alleged the papal nuncio would dress very discretely and wear a baseball cap pulled down to hide his face from anyone who might recognize him. Not many notable locals frequented the *malecon*, so it would be possible for the papal nuncio to go unnoticed there.

The area also attracted young homeless boys, mostly Haitian, who worked the area shining the shoes of tourists and hotel workers. Wesolowski would frequent the area and over time engaged several young boys in conversation, eventually building a relationship of trust with them. He then allegedly took them to discreet locations and offered them money to perform sexual acts or take off their clothes so he could see them naked.

The accusations about the papal nuncio's activities became public as a result of Piera's reporting, and it wasn't too long before he disappeared from the country. Deacon Francisco Javier Occi Reyes, who worked with Wesolowski, confirmed these activities when he himself was arrested on June 24, 2013, for soliciting sex from minors.

Following Piera's reporting, the papal nuncio stopped going to the waterfront and instead sent Reyes on his behalf to collect young boys for him. Unfortunately for Reyes the Church did not send anyone to bail him out, so on July 2, 2013, he sent a letter to Wesolowski and to the cardinal, which was obtained by the *New York Times*. In the letter, Reyes admitted to finding young boys for Wesolowski for the purposes of engaging in sexual activity. He sought forgiveness and hoped that Wesolowski would also pray for forgiveness for his depraved sexual appetite.

In addition to the papal nuncio's activities, the cardinal was also dealing with another priest who was involved in sexual activities with young boys, Wesolowski's good friend Father Wojciech (Alberto) Gil, another Catholic priest in the Dominican Republic. Gil was also under suspicion of molesting his alter boys and joining Wesolowski at his beach home with young boys for sexual escapades. Like Wesolowski, Gil also disappeared from the Dominican Republic.

Wesolowski secretly returned to Rome in late August 2013, instead of being arrested in the Dominican Republic and prosecuted for his crimes. Cardinal Rodríguez claimed not to have any knowledge of Wesolowski's whereabouts and referred to him as a "great friend" and "promoter of peace."

Let there be no mistake, the Dominican Republic is a small country, and secrets are not well kept. Public figures are fully exposed, and people talk. The cardinal's claim about not knowing the whereabouts of the papal nuncio was ridiculous. I have no doubt the cardinal knew exactly where the papal nuncio was, and furthermore, I highly suspect the cardinal arranged Wesolowski's "secret" departure from the country.

According to the Vatican, the cardinal should have reported these suspected crimes to local authorities, but that never happened. Instead, Wesolowski found refuge in the Vatican and was never held accountable for any of the alleged sexual crimes he committed in the Dominican Republic. This all took place before Wally and I arrived in the country, but that didn't stop the cardinal from using our presence as a diversion to not have to address these atrocities in the media. Eventually Attorney General Brito requested Wesolowski be extradited to the Dominican Republic to stand trial for his alleged sexual crimes. Not surprisingly, the Vatican claimed diplomatic immunity and refused the extradition request.

The Vatican assured the Dominican Republic justice system that Wesolowski would be tried in a Vatican court based on the evidence provided by the attorney general of the Dominican Republic. And evidence there was—according to multiple sources, Wesolowski had thousands of pornographic images of children on his computer, he had videotaped his sexual escapades, and of course there is the letter from Deacon Reyes to the cardinal and the papal nuncio admitting guilt. There was no reason that Wesolowski and Gil should not have been returned to the Dominican Republic, but the Vatican was not going to allow that to happen.

The situation unfortunately lost its appeal in the press for two reasons. First, there was a gay U.S. ambassador at the embassy and this was much more exciting to the gossip rags in the Dominican Republic than the sexcapades of a former papal nuncio. Second, the cardinal controlled most of the dissemination of the news and basically forbade the media from covering the issue.

In summer 2014, Monsignor Victor Masalles, who would later become a thorn in our side, was in Rome on Church business when, according to his Twitter account, he was surprised to see Wesolowski strolling along the Via Della Scrofa—a street in Rome. Wesolowski was supposed to be under house arrest in the Vatican.

Following this sighting, Wesolowski was confined to his Vatican apartment until the trial was to begin. The trial was initially set for July 2015 but was delayed because Wesolowski fell ill and was rushed to a Rome hospital.

On August 21, 2015, Wesolowski died in his Vatican apartment. According to reports, a friar who shared his residence discovered him at 5:00 a.m. sitting in front of his television. Reports indicate he died of natural causes.

So think about it...this is a man whom the Vatican and Cardinal Rodríguez went to great lengths to protect. There are suspicions they helped him escape the Dominican Republic and avoid prosecution in a secular court. They allowed him to roam freely and delayed his trial multiple times, and then ultimately he died in the comforts of the Vatican without standing trial for his crimes.

I am no conspiracy theorist, but I do find it extremely convenient that despite all the evidence, witnesses, letters, and video footage, the papal nuncio was never held accountable for his crimes. The Vatican avoided a scandalous trial. Maybe the comforts of a Vatican apartment aren't the most secure place to await trial after all.

Getting Schooled

During the Obama administration, the State Department and in particular USAID, supported a tremendous amount of educational programs globally. The president and the first lady were huge promoters of education both domestically and as a matter of foreign policy. While living in the Dominican Republic, my husband visited many public and private educational centers, all at the invitation of the schools. I also made my own visits to educational centers, sometimes alone at the school's invitation and sometimes accompanying my husband.

By spring 2016, we had developed a solid relationship with the business community in Santiago, the second largest city in the Dominican Republic. Santiago was also the location of one of the Bi-National Centers in the Dominican Republic. Bi-National Centers were educational facilities supported by the U.S. embassy that promoted and offered classes in English in cooperation with the local business community. We had visited the Bi-National Center practically every time we visited Santiago and had regular communications with business leaders who served on its board.

As a result of our obvious interest in education and the support of programs that provided opportunities for future generations, we were invited to attend a Model UN program at Instituto Iberia in Santiago.

I emphasize "we" because by this point almost all invitations to events that supported public interest were addressed and extended not only to the ambassador but to myself as well. My husband was very adamant that I attend events with him as a representative of the U.S. embassy and President Obama. This was his decision to make and I was happy to comply. There were, of course, exceptions, but in most cases I participated.

The program involved older, senior-level students who were studying the global diplomatic process. Although we heard many times from people how "honored" they were we attend this event or that event, the truth was we were the ones honored to participate in this program. By my definition, there is no greater equalizer on earth than education.

So in February 2016, we left Santo Domingo for the two-hour drive to Santiago. Usually we would be briefed on the way to an event, but for this event, the program was relatively straightforward. We knew Victor Martinez, the school's owner/director very well, and were already familiar with the program.

Victor greeted us upon our arrival and took us to a large classroom where the participating students were seated at desks configured in a large square around the room. Each student or student pair was seated at a desk with the name of the country they had chosen to represent. We were very impressed that the students had done their research on the countries they were representing and were familiar with the government structure and political hurdles those countries faced. We observed the interaction the students conducted based on the rules and procedures of the United Nations General Assembly and listened as they presented their various positions. Most private schools in the Dominican Republic teach some or all of their curriculums in English, unlike the public school system. Following the Model UN program, we toured the entire facility.

Following the tour, we were taken to a large open-air sports arena that doubled as a general assembly arena for the school. There was a large stage and rows of white chairs where we would hold a panel conversation with Victor to discuss international diplomacy. I don't recall how many students attended the general assembly but I clearly remember they were the older, more senior classes. Model UN program content is not exactly a subject matter for young students. After the panel concluded, the ambassador and I answered many questions from the students and then we adjourned. We shook a few hands, extended our thanks to Victor and the staff, and departed, feeling honored to have experienced such a successful day...or so we thought!

The next month, the religious community caught wind of our visit to Instituto Iberia and all hell broke loose. The country's Catholic and evangelical leaders went completely off the rails, accusing us of promoting our "gay agenda" and forcing our so-called nefarious influence upon their unsuspecting children to turn them gay. For the record, no one is influenced to be or is turned gay. The local media began publishing many articles indicating we were appearing at schools with the purpose of promoting same sex marriage and trying to mold young minds about our sinful ways. It definitely was one of the largest media controversies we ever experienced.

What really fed the firestorm was when newspapers plastered on their front pages a photo of us seated in a classroom with seven- and eight-year-olds. Indeed, we did attend a USAID program at a small country school for elementary-aged children, which had limited electricity and was looking for support to expand their facilities. Embassy staff had taken that picture because there were no press there that day. The purpose of our visit was to discuss with administrators how USAID resources could be used to assist the school in expanding the educational opportunities for its community. We had visited this school long before our visit to Instituto Iberia.

We had been touring the country school when one of the teachers—a young American—wanted the ambassador to see her classroom and meet her students. She was proud of the work she was doing there and was honored the ambassador and I had traveled to this mountain village to note the needs of her students. I was standing just outside the classroom with some of our embassy staff when as a courtesy I was extended an invitation to briefly engage with the teacher and her students. These children did not speak English and the embassy interpreter translated the few remarks the ambassador made to the students. The entire experience lasted five minutes; I was neither introduced as Wally's husband nor did I make any remarks. But somehow the media obtained the picture and fabricated a story of its own.

Clearly this was a manipulation on the part of those wishing to distort the truth and purpose of our visit. And it worked.

Unwelcome Hospitality

It didn't take long for the cardinal, Pastor Fidel Lorenzo of the Dominican Council of Evangelical Unity, and other religious leaders to have a complete meltdown over this portrayal by the media that we were pedophiles. Twitter and other social media outlets buzzed about our so-called "gay agenda."

The flames of the media firestorm were further fanned when Father Manuel Ruiz, the principal at St. John The Baptist College in Santo Domingo, erected a billboard-sized banner on the exterior wall of the school stating, "La Entrada del Senor Embajador de los Estados Unidos NO ESTA PERMITIDA En Este Instituto San Juan Bautista." In other words, "The U.S. ambassador is not permitted inside this institution." This display of "hospitality" made the cover of every newspaper in the country, was covered on every television and radio program, and even spread into the international media, including CNN and some outlets in Great Britain.

Shortly after the banner appeared, though, it was spray-painted—or should I say edited?—with a message questioning the intolerance of Father Ruiz. The night after the banner was vandalized Father Ruiz doubled down and erected a new banner high above the old one. I thought the money being used to erect these banners of hate could have been put to better use, but apparently Father Ruiz wanted to be sure that we understood that the ambassador, just in case he decided to drop by uninvited, was not welcome at the school.

But it wasn't just the Catholic Church and its representatives that wanted a piece of the action. Pastor Fidel Lorenzo managed to get in his five minutes of hate dissemination. He released a statement that the ambassador "is violating our law every time he visits a school with his husband," claiming that because the Dominican Republic is officially a Christian country, it was prohibited for the ambassador and me to visit any school, even if invited by the school administrators, because it violated the values of Christian teachings. I am not exactly sure what Lorenzo speculated we were doing when visiting these facilities or why these visits were of specific interest to him, but clearly Pastor Lorenzo was harboring some impure thoughts.

We had been visiting educational facilities practically since the day we arrived. Our first visit to the city of Santiago was hosted by Monsignor Agripino Nunez, the most prominent leader of the Catholic Church next to the cardinal himself and Rector of Pontificia Universidad Catolica Madre y Maestra in Santiago, the most prominent Catholic University in the Dominican Republic. You would have thought if the cardinal were going to have a fit over our visiting any school it would have been his own Catholic University. I also had visited a secondary educational facility in a small *batey* community just outside Esperanza in the northwest part of the Dominican Republic. It was not an official U.S. embassy visit, although I did meet with our Peace Corps volunteer stationed in that area. I promoted the visit via social media and there was not a single response from the religious community. I only assume that they didn't mind me visiting a school in a community where people had to bathe in sewage-filled rivers and lived without electricity and running water.

This public fiasco didn't die a normal slow media death as most of these situations had in the past. It seemed to be the platform Lorenzo decided to use to forward his own agenda of hate and discrimination. And he had no shortage of platforms in which to spread his messages. Lorenzo receives a lot of international support for his ministries in the Dominican Republic; one of his partners is evangelical minister Franklin Graham, son of televangelist Billy Graham, in the United States. I have no doubt the children they serve through Operation Christmas Child brings a great deal of light and joy to the lives of the young people who benefit from their generosity. However, that is not the only goal of their ministries. Lorenzo doesn't just preach the gospel and obviously neither does Graham. Both men use their pulpits to influence and insert themselves into government policy both in the United States and the Dominican Republic. Religious institutions are not supposed to use tax-free donations in the United States for political purposes; however, religious organizations in the Dominican Republic are very involved in influencing government policy. Graham spends a considerable amount of tax-free money supporting institutions globally that influence the governments and legal institutions of foreign countries, and this is no less the case in the Dominican Republic. Personally I don't have a problem with Graham expressing his right to use his organization's money for this reason, but I do have a problem with it being tax-free. This is a direct violation of the separation of church and state, which is a foundational pillar of a transparent democracy. But I digress!

A few days following the media frenzy over the banner at St. John The Baptist College, Lorenzo launched a public campaign using the White House website to promote a petition to force the White House to withdraw my husband as the U.S. ambassador. He had already demanded that President Medina deem my husband as "persona non grata"—which would have effectively forced us out of the country— to no avail. During the entire tenure of our service in the Dominican Republic, President Medina never once engaged with the media in a negative way regarding my husband. Conversely, he was silent if not supportive on the matter, which I am sure drove the cardinal, Lorenzo, and other religious leaders completely nuts.

Lorenzo entered more than 30,000 signatures on the White House petition demanding the removal of my husband as ambassador. When you have the money to pay people to sit in the offices of your church entering the names of your congregation on a petition, then no doubt it would gain a little steam. The entire situation was complete nonsense; his petition could have listed a million names and my husband would not have been removed. However, it did manage to get a response from Washington. U.S. National Security Advisor to President Obama Susan Rice released a statement in response to the calls for my husband to be removed:

> President Obama chose Ambassador Brewster to represent the United States government in the Dominican Republic because of his outstanding credentials, integrity and dedication to the advancing the interests of this country. He has the full support of this President, this White House and the entire U.S. government and I know he will continue to advocate tirelessly for the interests of the United States in the Dominican Republic.

I know my husband was very proud that President Obama's administration was in full support of his work and initiatives on behalf of the U.S. government; however, on some level I have no doubt he was irritated that the conversation needed to happen in the first place.

Celebrating Terrorism

In early summer 2016, it was time for a short relaxing weekend before the kickoff of the OAS General Assembly meetings that were being held in Santo Domingo June 13–15. We went to sleep on Saturday night feeling confident because everything was in place for the following week. Sunday morning was my favorite time of the week. Living in a foreign country, I found news from the States was not always immediate. But the first thing I did every Sunday morning was turn on my favorite news programs, CBS Sunday Morning, Meet the Press, and Face the Nation.

What greeted me that morning was breaking news from a local Florida station of the shooting at Pulse, a gay nightclub in Orlando. This would turn out to be the worst mass shooting in American history as well as a specific hate crime against the LGBT community and the worst terrorist attack on U.S. soil since September 11, 2001. Wally and I were stunned, as was the entire nation of the United States. It wasn't long before Wally's phone started ringing because everyone would be preparing for alternative measures as a result of any schedule changes with the principals from Washington and their pending visits the next day.

Shock and sadness gripped us all. I stayed glued to the television as the details unfolded about the number of people who were injured, missing, or dead.

Because the OAS meetings would be starting the next day, there were many different groups that wished to express their agendas to the member states that would be attending. In the Dominican Republic, the religious institutions, specifically the Catholic and evangelical communities, always had a political agenda they wished to impose on emerging democracies. As a result of our presence in the country, many LGBT groups had found a platform on which to express their desire for human equality and to raise awareness of the discrimination they suffered as a result of the bigoted policies of the Church. It wasn't the government of the Dominican Republic that systematically promoted polices of bigotry and discrimination; it was the Catholic and evangelical churches that exerted their influence in the government that instituted these hurdles for equality. The OAS meetings would be a world stage where they could raise a lot of attention to their cause.

At this stage in our tenure Cardinal Rodríguez had been retired, in fact no one had heard from him in the media since the previous December when he criticized my husband for raising the issues of corruption in the business community and referred to him as a "wife" who should stay home and do the housework.

At this point, the self-anointed man at the helm was Monsignor Victor Masalles. He was no stranger to the influences of the media and clearly loved his moments in the spotlight. In response to the OAS meetings, Masalles organized a religious march calling for the institutional discrimination against the equality of LGBT people. The OAS had placed on their agenda a resolution calling for the recognition of the rights of LGBT people during their assembly to be held that week.

Clearly this did not sit well with Masalles. He organized a march and provided transportation for thousands of people from across the country to the capital city. Typically, the Church pays these attendees a small stipend and provides food for the day in return for their attendance, so in a country where most people live in extreme poverty, it is not difficult to recruit attendance for these types of activities with very little investment. We were aware this event had been scheduled but assumed that the protest would be rescheduled as a result of the Orlando terrorist attack. This was not the case.

Masalles proceeded with his protest against the equality of LGBT people despite the fact they were still pulling bodies from the Orlando nightclub and notifying families of their losses. We were truly shocked; we refused to believe that anyone—specifically a man of the cloth—could be so heartless. So we decided to see for ourselves. We thought if this were going to take place it was something the ambassador should witness with his own eyes.

The ambassador's personal security detail was home because it was Sunday and we had not scheduled any public appearances that day. Wally called his head bodyguard and notified his head of diplomatic security that we would be taking a drive to see if the protest would actually be happening. Once the ambassador's security detail arrived at the CMR, we drove to the offices of the foreign ministry where the protest was scheduled, and what we saw moved my husband to tears. There they were, hundreds of buses, thousands of people all wearing white carrying signs of hate and calling for discrimination of a community who had just suffered one of the most notable terrorist attacks in history.

They were not organizing to pray for the victims. They were not asking God to provide peace and comfort for those who had lost loved ones. They were not praying for the souls of those who had lost their lives. They were literally celebrating and calling for further discrimination against these very people, and in a few cases their very own. There were Dominicans who had been murdered in Orlando as well, and their family members in the Dominican Republic were dealing with the pain of their losses or awaiting news of their death. I can only imagine how they must have felt when they turned on their televisions to see Father Masalles promoting hate against those whom they had just lost.

Spring 2016 proved to be one of the most turbulent times during our tenure in the Dominican Republic. A lot of our goals were coming to fruition and as our success began to gain steam, so did the opposition. I can be somewhat naïve at times as to the motivation of religious leaders who disseminate hate. As my husband and I both have indicated numerous times, we are men of faith, we believe in God, and we do our best to follow the teachings of Christ. Obviously, I understand there are disingenuous men and women who claim to be people of faith but instead promote division as a position to obtain control over a group of people. I still want to believe that they truly know that is wrong—or do they?

The cardinal, Lorenzo, and Masalles are a prime examples of those who used our notoriety to get their names in—or out!—of the paper.

Their tactics and attempts were nothing new to us and were certainly nothing that would warrant a response from either of us. We knew no good would result from a meeting with the cardinal, despite the fact he never would have extended an invitation in the first place. He actually demanded that I never be allowed on Church property. As for the evangelical community, we would have been more than happy to have had a conversation had we been extended an invitation to do so. Once, while serving on a panel during a radio program, I was asked by an evangelical pastor if I would have a meeting with the leaders of his religious community. The question was in response to me being asked about my faith. I responded that I would more than happy to join them for coffee and a conversation—but the invitation never came.

The ambassador did, however, have personal conversations with Vice President Biden, UN Ambassador Samantha Power, and several others about the Catholic Church and its hostility toward us. I feel certain some of those messages were appropriately delivered to the Vatican. Vice President Biden actually had a personal conversation about the matter when he visited the pope, and Senator Durbin wrote the following letter of concern and delivered it to the pope on December 15, 2015, through diplomatic channels.

His Holiness, Pope Francis
Apostolic Palace
00120 Vatican City

December 15, 2015

Most Holy Father Pope Francis,

Thank you for your recent visit to Washington and address to our Joint Session of Congress. Your visit and message had a profound impact on all of us.

I write to you about a matter involving Cardinal Nicolas de Jesus Lopez Rodriguez of the Archdiocese of Santo Domingo in the Dominican Republic and the United States Ambassador to that country, Wally Brewster.

Ambassador Brewster is from my state of Illinois and he is a personal friend. I supported President Obama's selection of Ambassador Brewster and he was sworn into his position in my Senate office. Ambassador Brewster is gay and was married under the laws of the United States to his partner, Bob Satawake.

Even before Ambassador Brewster's arrival in Santo Domingo in 2013, Cardinal Rodriguez launched a personal attack against him with public statements quoted in the popular press. The Cardinal used the hateful slur "faggot," which he continues to use to this day. In a recent interview Cardinal Rodriguez again described the Ambassador as a "faggot" and falsely claimed the Ambassador was setting out to promote "faggotry" in the Dominican Republic. The Cardinal described the Ambassador as a "wife" who "should stick to housework."

In the past the Cardinal and Dominican Church leaders even organized a "Black Monday" public protest against the Ambassador. Their action led to a counter-demonstration in support of the Ambassador and his partner.

Despite these hateful words and personal attacks, Ambassador Brewster has worked to quiet the conflict between Church leaders and himself. His patience and professionalism in light of these mean-spirited attacks by the Cardinal demonstrate his personal commitment to his responsibility of representing the United States of America.

The Church's teachings on gay marriage are well known but the Church also teaches us to show tolerance for those with different sexual orientations. The intolerant public statements of Cardinal Rodriguez are inconsistent with that clearly stated value.

Since your selection as Pope, you have shared a message of compassion, tolerance, and love. I remember distinctly when you spoke to us at the joint session of Congress in September and reminded us of our responsibility to "defend and preserve the dignity of your fellow citizens in the tireless and demanding pursuit of the common good."

I accept that challenge and I am calling on you to ask nothing less of the hierarchy of the Church.

Sincerely,

Richard J. Durbin
United States Senator

I still question what the cardinal, Lorenzo, and Masalles thought could be gained from a public fight with the U.S. ambassador who was the de facto representative of the U.S. government in the Dominican Republic. My husband was extraordinarily popular. We couldn't be at any event or go anywhere in public throughout the entire country without him being asked for photographs. Wally is a wonderful human being; he is extremely genuine and truly cares for all mankind. No doubt people recognized this in him because he was embraced publicly at every turn. He never once spoke publicly about the cardinal, Lorenzo, Masalles, or any other religious leader. He refused to engage with such rhetoric, but they kept coming and they kept believing that somehow publicly bullying my husband was going to benefit them. I don't believe it ever had any positive effect on their causes, but to this day it remains the modus operandi of people like this—when they need to get attention they find someone to pick on.

Following the Orlando shooting and the evangelical church's last effort to shame the LGBT community, the opposition finally lost its steam. We served out the remainder of our time in the Dominican Republic tying up loose ends and making plans to return to the private sector; this era of our government service was coming to an end and we were ready to explore new adventures. I don't often find much affirmation with Fox News but it published an article, "Gay U.S. Ambassador Has Helped LGBT Rights Movement in the Dominican Republic," which was filled with praise by members of the local LGBT community and recognition of my husband's work by the U.S. organization Human Rights First. No matter what you do in life there will always be someone or some group who will oppose change, but when you attempt to promote change in the humanitarian sector that opposition can become extreme. Your only option is to keep your eyes forward.

9: Unearthing Corruption

The investment opportunities in the Dominican Republic are prolific. The American Chamber of Commerce is well organized, and the leaders of the business community are highly educated and exude an entrepreneurial spirit. Developing partnerships and direct investment, however, in the current infrastructure requires investors to maneuver extremely difficult hurdles of corruption.

The monopolistic style and protectionism measures in place make it virtually impossible for foreign investment opportunity and as a result the current marketplace is becoming stagnant. The Central Bank and the government of the Dominican Republic will argue that the current growth in the economy has exceed 5 percent in recent years but in reality, this is a result of Venezuelan monetary investment, including drug-related and money-laundering activities, which was stolen from the Venezuelan people under the dictatorship of Hugo Chavez. These resources have been funneled into the Dominican Republic economy through excessive construction of condos and office complexes. Government leaders and elected officials are often paid handsomely to provide illegal permits or to simply look the other way.

In the 2016 election, well-known *senador* Felix Bautista, named one of the most corrupt politicians in the world by Transparency International, was re-elected to the congress by a huge majority. He was exonerated by the judicial system for corrupt practices against the government for stealing tax dollars and extorting the private sector for payment in return for government contracts. According to sources, Bautista's net worth in 1996 was $39,000, probably not even enough to qualify for a visitor's visa to the United States. By 2010, after serving a few years in appointed positions within the Dominican government, his wealth grew to $54.1 million.

According to the judicial system of the Dominican Republic, there is no proof he was involved in any illegal activity or used his position within the government to leverage a monetary benefit. It is well known that the general population will sell their voting identification for as little as 250 pesos on election day or to the highest bidder. These types of transparent corrupt activities destroy any comfort level a foreign investor might consider.

The Golden Ticket

The U.S. visa is the most coveted document a Dominican citizen can possess short of their own country's passport. In fact, approximately 1.5 million Dominican citizens have immigrated to the United States, leaving their homeland and Dominican passport behind for a new home and new opportunity in America, so I suppose on some levels a U.S. visa or passport is more desirable than their birthright.

More than 10 percent of the population has immigrated, and there are many more who want to follow in their footsteps. In 2015, the U.S. embassy issued 80,000 immigrant visas to Dominican citizens—a path to a new life in America. If this were to continue, it would take fewer than 20 years to drain the entire population of the Dominican Republic.

For many Dominicans, though, the opportunity to immigrate or even obtain a visa to visit the United States will never happen. The U.S. embassy processes and interviews approximately 1,200 people per day requesting a travel visa to the United States. Some applicants are applying for student visas, some request a basic visitor visa, some seek medical treatment, and others wish to move to the United States to be with family members.

Of all these requests, the basic visitor visa is the most commonly denied. More than 50 percent of the B1/B2 visa requests (tourist visa) are denied. The approval process for a tourist visa is extremely subjective and most Dominicans who apply are ill-prepared for the process and interview. Those who can save enough money for the application fee, which in many cases is one month's salary, don't have a substantiated reason for their visit. United States citizens are never subjected to this type of scrutiny when deciding where or when they will travel or for what purpose. Most Dominicans do not have a bank account, do not own a home, do not own a car, and if employed have jobs that pay as little as $200–$300 per month. Give that some thought.

One of the largest employers in the Dominican Republic is the National Police, with a starting salary of less than $200 per month and with very little opportunity for advancement. When people with few resources can scrape together enough money for the application process and interview for a tourist visa, they are most likely going to be denied.

It makes me wonder, do we systematically discriminate against poor people? On many levels we probably do. We ask, how is it that they can take their family of four to Disneyland when they only make $200 per month? The answer is they have saved for years to afford the plane tickets and will stay with family members. They won't be eating in fancy restaurants or flying first class. They simply want an opportunity to visit family they have not seen in years and show their children an example of a better life. How come they have not seen their family in the United States? Those family members most likely overstayed their visas and can't return to the Dominican Republic without ever being able to return the United States again.

Then there is the better life. Once in the United States, they can find almost any job that will pay more than $200 per month. They can put their kids in a public school, which provides a far better education than they can ever receive in the public schools of the Dominican Republic. They can be with family members that in some cases they have been separated from for decades. Would you go back? Those are the questions our foreign service officers have to ask themselves when reviewing visa applications.

These are fair assessments, but what about those who are truly genuine in their desire to visit the United States, expose their family and children to a different culture and a different way of living? Is it fair that they are guilty by association to their fellow countrymen who have gamed the system and ruined it for them? No! But, then life is not fair.

Largely, our foreign service officers do an exemplary job with the few resources they are allotted from Congress. They are understaffed and work diligently to be as observational as possible when representing our country and our values abroad.

Then there are the wealthy applicants who feel the U.S. embassy is nothing more than a visa ATM for them and their family, friends, and colleagues. The Dominican Republic is not a cheap place to live.

Real estate rivals the best of America's major cities, electricity costs 30 times more than in the United States, and gasoline is double the cost. Energy is an immense hurdle for Caribbean nations; they do not have natural resources or the infrastructure to support wind and solar energy; however, that is slowly changing despite certain levels of resistance to new technologies. Where they do have the infrastructure, the monopolistic hurdles set in place by the uber-wealthy keep out any opportunity for alternative energy policies.

I had opportunities to meet and socialize with the private sector elite and the political influencers during my time in the Dominican Republic. It took a long time for me to understand the reasons behind the day-to-day decisions made by the uber-wealthy in a country where they, in some cases, had more money than the government itself controlled. The Dominican Republic is basically controlled by a small community of extremely wealthy people who do a great deal of good trying to provide greater opportunities for those less fortunate. But the corrupt practices of many elected government officials in the country make it impossible for them or anyone to be transparent.

Secrets are not well-kept in the Dominican Republic except those about personal wealth. Everyone, regardless of social status, hides their money or some portion of it, and I can't blame them. After long-serving dictator Rafael Trujillo was assassinated in 1961, democracy surfaced but has only been in existence since the 1970s. There are a handful of good politicians in the Dominican Republic and I was able to meet them privately and discuss the future of their country with them. When the opportunity presented itself I even advised them on some levels—who knows if my advice was heeded or not!

The few good politicians deserve a great deal of credit for maneuvering in a world of totally corrupt practices. Somehow they do the job they were elected or appointed to do despite facing brick walls at every turn. Most elected officials in the Dominican Republic have taken the opportunity to pass legislation strictly for self-serving purposes and over time have created an environment where they can rip off the public and private enterprises with impunity.

In countries like the Dominican Republic, developing democracies are faced with hurdles that most western nations can't comprehend. It may be fair to pose the question why not vote these corrupt officials out of office, but the answer is not that simple. The Dominican Republic has one of the worst public education systems in the world and as a result there are not a lot of choices when electing government leaders. That is not to say all the elected leaders or appointed officials are corrupt or not genuine. President Medina is taking extreme measures to overhaul the public education system and provide legitimate access to all Dominicans to a proper education. He faces many hurdles in his endeavors. Hopefully for the country, his initiatives regarding education will pay off and history will be kind to his legacy.

I will always be grateful to President Medina and First Lady Cándida Medina for their incredible kindness and public extension of their friendship and cooperation, not only with my husband but with me as well. Their support gave me comfort that the efforts of the "Christian" community that called for our expulsion fell flat.

The Underbelly of Major League Baseball

When flying into or out of Santo Domingo, planes fly over some of the most beautiful baseball facilities you could lay eyes on. These mirror the professional fields you see when attending a major league baseball (MLB) game in the United States. There is a reason for that: they *are* MLB facilities. Virtually every MLB team in the United States has a farm facility in the Dominican Republic. Baseball is a major economic commodity of trade between the United States and the Dominican Republic, and the sport generates a colossal amount of revenue for both countries. It is no secret that Dominican baseball players have had great influence over the years in the development and popularity of the sport in the United States.

I have had the wonderful privilege of knowing personally many Dominican professional baseball players and still maintain many of those friendships. These men provide hope to young men in the most impoverished communities throughout their country, inspiring them to reach beyond their surroundings for a better life through baseball. For a few it is a dream come true: achieving a MLB contract, a life in the United States, millions of dollars, and most importantly freedom to travel the world, to access and open otherwise closed doors, and to provide for their families who sacrificed so much for them. It is a beautiful story, and one we hear over and over again from the sports announcers who speak of the hurdles these young men have overcome each time they swing a bat or make a dramatic catch at the fence line of a MLB park.

My personal connection to baseball began on July 30, 2003, when I moved next door to Moises Alou in Chicago. I was always a fan of baseball, but never had the talent for it—tennis was really my game. I loved to watch baseball, though, and would attend games in college as often as I could. After moving next door to the Alous, we became close friends, and we often joined them at Cubs games in Chicago. I spent many afternoons sitting with Austria in the family section of MLB ballparks watching Moises play. Particularly memorable was the year Moises was on a hot streak and each time he would hit a home run, Austria and I would get a bottle of champagne if we were at the game. We attended many games that season, and Moises hit a lot of home runs. It is what I would call a win-win.

From 2003 until Moises' retirement, Wally and I joined Austria at more baseball games than I can remember, including flying to San Francisco when he signed for three seasons with the Giants and to New York when he played the last games of his career with the Mets. We attended the last cross-town series between the Mets and the Yankees and rode the team bus from Mets stadium to the old Yankee stadium for the last game the two teams would ever play before that stadium was torn down and replaced by the current Yankee stadium. There are so many amazing memories and experiences, and I will cherish them forever.

When Wally became the U.S. ambassador in the Dominican Republic, we were very excited that we would have opportunities to attend winter ball games in the Dominican Republic. Most people don't realize that many professional baseball players play year-round. They play for MLB teams in the U.S. during the regular season, and many play winter ball for professional teams in the Dominican Republic, Puerto Rico, Venezuela, Mexico, and even Japan. Experiencing baseball in the Dominican Republic is a little different than at a major league park in the U.S. To begin they have cheerleaders who perform on top of the dugouts between innings, pitching changes, or any other type of delay. Suffice it to say some of their performances and scant uniforms would make a sailor blush.

The energy level is frenetic and the fans are zealous. The spectators in the Dominican Republic are experts in the game and they show no mercy to a player who makes an error or to an umpire with whose call they disagree. Getting kicked out of a ballpark in the Dominican Republic for loudly voicing one's opinion is akin to getting kicked out of church for praying: it's not going to happen.

Although I bristled at the behavior of some of the fans, I relished in the culture, passion, and knowledge of the game. Baseball is an integral part of the relationship between the United States and the Dominican Republic, and culturally we engaged diplomatically with many organizations that promoted this relationship. We were invited to opening day ceremonies and the recognition of Dominican players at MLB parks in the U.S., and we were present for almost every MLB and player event that took place in the Dominican Republic. We hosted MLB events at our home in Santo Domingo and broadened our friendship with many professional players including Robinson Cano, David Ortiz, Julio Lugo, Nelson Cruz, Aramis Ramirez, and many more.

There are many Dominican players who achieve success in the MLB and contribute to organizations that provide for those less fortunate. Some even develop foundations that provide the disenfranchised with hope and access to a better life. But this is limited in scope because only a small percentage of those who pursue a career in professional baseball ever get to swing a bat in a MLB ballpark.

Tragically, there is a dark side to major league baseball, a dreadful story rarely told at the ballparks but one I was able to witness personally. As we traveled throughout the Dominican Republic during our diplomatic mission, it was hard to miss that baseball was the core fabric of the land. Every single town, village, and even some *bateyes* we visited had a baseball field. They may not have mirrored the professional fields we saw when taking off or landing in Santo Domingo, but they are there, and they are the cornerstone of the community. These ballparks provide hope and inspiration to young men—heartbreakingly in most cases, a false hope.

We play the lottery because someone wins, but the odds are stacked against us. These young men play baseball not to win, but to live. Scouts look for talent in the dusty fields of the rural communities where boys as young as eight years old play. This is no secret and these communities know when the scouts are around. Many scouts are not affiliated with MLB or the professional clubs of the Dominican Republic, but know they can ride the gravy train if they find one kid with the right talent to make it to the MLB.

If a young man is good enough, he will be accepted into a training camp owned by one of the major league teams in the U.S. There he will enter a development program at the academy to develop his skills in the hope that one day he is given an opportunity in the big leagues. Next is where this begins to get ugly. To be admitted to a major league camp, he needs to be 16 years old. At this tender age, these young men leave their families and school and enter a camp where they will train full-time. However, many times these young men are not 16 years old—if they have a recognized talent from a legitimate scout, a birth certificate easily can be falsified.

What's the harm? The educational system in a rural community in the Dominican Republic is limited at best and barely provides students with basic reading and math skills. When a young man enters the academy, he leaves his formal educational program and is subjected to hours of baseball practice with very little educational emphasis.

My husband had multiple conversations with owners of MLB teams, the MLB Players Association, and the executives at MLB in New York and in the Dominican Republic to encourage a cooperative effort to ensure these young men are provided with a basic education during their time in these major league camps. Unfortunately, the effort in this arena never produced any quantitative result. It is truly a humanitarian crisis that we as a democracy contribute to. Thousands of young men are recruited into these camps with the unrealizable hope and dream of becoming a MLB player, only to be eventually escorted to the street without an education and at an age where the only future ahead is a life of poverty and shining shoes. It's ugly and true; undoubtedly my words will anger many in positions of influence affiliated with MLB, but the truth sometimes makes people mad.

It doesn't have to be this way. The U.S.-based companies that own MLB organizations should be required to provide a proper education to the young men who are recruited into their camps. Removing a child from the only educational opportunity he may ever have and then returning him to the streets with no life skills in a country where there is little hope for success is unconscionable. It's just plain wrong and can be fixed with a little cooperative effort from the influencers and owners in MLB.

So next time you are at a MLB park and a Dominican player hits a home run, remember that there are thousands of young men just like him in the baseball clubs in the Dominican Republic who sacrificed their education and future who never made it to the plate.

10: Building Diplomatic Friendships

Every ambassador's spouse is as different as every ambassador, and depending on various factors and personal passions, each will operate very differently in his or her role. The one constant was the support we provided to each other. Social media allowed us a platform to communicate in a private format where we could exchange ideas, encouragement, or rants about the various situations we faced.

Despite my ability to throw a good party, that wasn't my focus or my purpose in the Dominican Republic. I am passionate about people, specifically marginalized people. I care about their opportunities, their health, their families and children, their access to justice and democracy, and their education, equality, and safety. I just want to leave the world a better place than I found it. It may sound extraordinarily Pollyanna, but it is my passion.

After we had solidified relationships with the government, and the diplomatic and private sectors of the country during our first year of service, we were feeling comfortable enough to continue moving the initiatives of President Obama forward. Wally, as ambassador, was deeply involved in priorities that were imperative to protect our shared national security interests, including drug and human trafficking. These activities were classified top secret, and my clearance did not allow me to be privy to the details of such initiatives. There were multiple departments involved in these bilateral activities, and they are ongoing today. It is extremely important that we continue to participate collectively with our partner countries in Latin America on these opportunities to shut down criminal enterprises.

After the initial shock of the U.S. ambassador being gay and married to a man had subsided, I began to focus on various humanitarian initiatives, including gender-based violence, child pregnancy, public health, and LGBT issues. We had met with virtually every significant leader in the government—even the president—and had engaged with the leaders of prominent educational institutions, including Monsignor Agripino Nunez. Monsignor Nunez never failed to attend our Fourth of July celebration. We were very public throughout the social scene of Santo Domingo and were comfortable with the progress we had made.

The general population began to view us as two men who worked for the U.S. government "just doing our jobs."

An opportunity arose for me to attend the opening of a new HIV clinic, but it was in one of *those* areas where we were prohibited from going. I went anyway. Being poor is not a disease, and sometimes, believe it or not, it can't be helped. I love the idea that the American dream exists— the notion that anyone, regardless of their circumstances, can pull themselves up by the bootstraps and make a life for themselves, but the reality is this is just not true for many. Most cannot pull themselves out of poverty, and this is especially true outside the United States in places where there isn't educational infrastructure or social platforms to assist the impoverished. Some people are just screwed. It isn't their fault, and unfortunately in this scenario life is just not fair.

I spent most of my time in the Dominican Republic working in marginalized communities. I was able to find resources to support programs that helped put food on the tables of the impoverished, support organizations that provided infrastructure and education, helped women obtain access to justice when they had been beaten by their husbands, and addressed issues of child pregnancy—and I do mean child. The Dominican Republic suffers from the highest rate of child pregnancy of any country in the Western Hemisphere. I define the term child as any person under the legal age of consent. You will hear the term teen pregnancy, and they may be 13 or 14 years old, but they are still children. This happens as a result of poverty combined with a lack of morality. The young girls typically come from impoverished homes with single mothers and adult men offer to pay for food and housing for their family if they can have sex with their daughters. These are supposedly Christian men who are almost always married with a family of their own. These young girls are not getting pregnant by teenage boys in their communities. There are a lot of NGOs in the Dominican Republic that are providing resources to help these communities provide a better life for their children.

There were a lot of great organizations that also provided other types of life-building improvements in the Dominican Republic. A gentleman with whom I became good friends ran an organization that provided free hearing assessments and free hearing aids to the hearing impaired. I was able to introduce him to our CDC country director and we attended an event where their patients were able to receive an assessment, be fitted for hearing aids, and taught how to use them. When you are born into a country that does not have a medical infrastructure to address the health concerns of the deaf, you really have no opportunity for any type of life. If you lose your hearing and don't have money to buy hearing aids, you will lose your job, your income, your home, and in some cases even your family. Foreign policy is about a lot more than trade deals; it is about humanitarian initiative and extending the hand of the United States of America to those in need. By allowing the marginalized access to democracy and providing a pathway for emerging democracies to join us on a global stage, we all help one another reach our full potential.

Going All In with Aid Initiatives

I had the opportunity to work on several human rights initiatives and public health policies while I was in the Dominican Republic. It never would have been possible if not for the cooperation of Dr. Nelson Arboleda, the CDC country director; Alexi Panehal, USAID country director; Ken Seifert, a career foreign service officer with USAID who coordinated multiple projects not only for USAID Dominican Republic but throughout the entire region; and Luis Duran, the liaison for the LGBT community. Alexi was a tour de force, all of five feet tall, with a strong will and an open mind. I loved her immediately, and she allowed me to be involved in as many USAID projects for which I had time. I was embraced by many in the embassy and provided opportunities to participate in their various initiatives. Dr. Arboleda and Alexi, however, went above and beyond to include me, and we collectively achieved extraordinary results.

Building Justice

Alexi was very proactive on issues that impacted women, specifically impoverished women. I could relate to this on a personal level, having grown up poor and the youngest of four kids, and raised in an environment influenced by a woman. I learned early on that the challenges women face in life because of their gender far exceed anything a man experiences. The Dominican Republic is not a place where women are respected and in too many cases they are physically abused by their husbands or boyfriends with little or no legal recourse. When I lived in the Dominican Republic, if a woman wanted to file a physical abuse complaint against a man, she had to do so in person at the National Police facility in Santo Domingo. If a woman lived in a rural community without access to transportation, how was she supposed to file a complaint? Certain parts of the Dominican Republic can be a four- to six-hour bus ride from the capital city. Women suffering these abuses in remote communities far from Santo Domingo certainly can't afford a bus ticket or a place to stay, and don't have the ability to fill out a report. The Dominican Republic suffers from the highest rate of gender-based violence per capita in the Western Hemisphere as a result.

Under Alexi's direction, USAID began funding Justices Houses in small, rural communities outside the major cities. The Justices Houses were staffed with attorneys and volunteers who provided counseling and assistance to those suffering from gender-based violence as well as offered other accesses to justice they may have needed. I visited several Justice Houses and many other projects funded by USAID. USAID receives its funding from the U.S. Congress and it is important to provide feedback to members of Congress so they clearly understand the importance of what is being accomplished in foreign countries where we maintain projects. I was able to provide a direct line of feedback to Washington through the relationships I maintained.

This type of foreign diplomacy is important in securing allies and establishing democracy around the world. The United States is a very powerful and influential player on the global scale, but we still need friends. The best way to develop friendships in diplomatic circles is to offer your hand first, provide a path for emerging democracies to feel secure, and provide leadership and in some cases financial resources to secure an infrastructure for them in which they can base their future. One thing is certain, if the United States doesn't extend that hand, foreign powers with nefarious intentions will extend their hand and that, my friends, is not good for the United States and not good for democracy.

Supporting the LGBT Community

In addition to Alexi, Luis, and Ken, there were Gary Lowman and Brock McCormack from the consular section. Gary was a career diplomat, and Brock was his "trailing spouse," a term I always considered derogatory, but that is what the State Department referred to these non-career U.S. employees who were married to a career diplomat.

They took the time to expose me to the projects that were in the works. Then they shared ideas they had that would require outside resources or funding from USAID that wasn't yet available. The first thing we did was to meet some of the program directors in communities where USAID was working. I met with members from the Dominican Republic's attorney general's office who were working on a justice program that provided access to justice in marginalized communities. I met with members of the police to discuss more effective ways to provide victims of crime an opportunity to ensure they received appropriate action on their complaints. I met with and toured agricultural facilities where farmers received assistance on how to be more efficient and produce better quality products, as well as members of the coffee clusters who needed support due to the difficulties they faced in rising costs and lack of land due to deforestation. Some of these initiatives ran pretty seamlessly but others required a more complex approach and were initiatives that eventually would become self-sustaining.

I was more keen to work on short-term initiatives because our time in the Dominican Republic was limited and I wanted to see the fruits of my labor. We worked closely with the LGBT community and through Gary and Luis set up a meeting with the leaders of the LGBT organizations in the country. There were a lot of people in the embassy who had huge reservations about our exposure and participation in the LGBT community. Before we arrived, DCM Dan Foote even made a comment in the press indicating that Wally was not coming to the Dominican Republic as an "activist for the gay community," but as the ambassador. Dan was absolutely correct, and under the circumstances it was the right thing to say, but it left an impression with the ultra conservatives and certain members of the private sector that we would ignore the LGBT community. When we engaged with the leaders a few short weeks after arriving it raised some serious eyebrows within our public affairs department.

We invited various LGBT organizations' leaders to our house for a coffee, and following the advice of a few in the embassy who expressed concern, we agreed there would not be any press coverage or photographs. This was the first time in the history of the diplomatic relationship between the Dominican Republic and the United States that members of the gay community had been officially, yet un-officially, invited to the residence of the U.S. ambassador. We had a wonderful conversation and primarily were interested in their challenges and concerns. We listened as each guest talked about their needs and hurdles and what they thought we could do to help make life better for their community.

The meeting was scheduled for one hour, and at the end we walked them to the door of the residence to say goodbye. Someone asked if they could take a selfie with the ambassador and me in our formal entry hall, which housed the U.S. and Dominican flags. Of course, we obliged and took several un-official photos in front of the flags and shook hands as they left. The next day there was a picture in the newspaper that had been lifted from social media claiming the ambassador had turned the U.S. embassy into a haven for gay people. It was absolutely ridiculous. I thought if you are going to blame me for something or accuse me of a certain position that I didn't promote, then why not promote it? It was clear at that point the media were going to attack my husband on any initiative he championed for the LGBT community, regardless of how small.

Diplomacy and Public Health

Dr. Nelson Arboleda gave me the opportunity to assist him in raising awareness about the mission of the CDC and the projects they were accomplishing under his direction. There are numerous deadly diseases floating around the world and it is the ultimate job of the CDC to ensure they don't make their ways to the shores of the United States. There is also a large humanitarian component to CDC's initiatives, such as supporting HIV and other sexually transmitted disease treatment. This is important because as people travel, so do the diseases they carry. Providing counseling and assistance to those who are being treated for communicable diseases highly reduces the chance of them spreading the diseases. I began speaking on behalf of the CDC and attended many events with Dr. Arboleda to help raise awareness of his section's work in the Dominican Republic. Ultimately I gave a presentation entitled "Public Health and Diplomacy" on the importance of why we engage with such initiatives outside the United States and the impact it has on our country's health safety. I was honored when Dr. Arboleda asked me to be his guest lecturer at a course he was teaching at the University of Miami Miller School of Medicine about my work with him in the Dominican Republic.

Experiencing the *Batey*

The Dominican Republic is not short on marginalized people—but thankfully, not short on people who work to help them. I met Gerald McElroy, a 28-year-old Yale and Columbia alumnus with an enormous passion for humanitarian initiatives, at the American Chamber of Commerce monthly luncheon. He was on the board of a student organization at Yale that supported a *batey* in the northern part of the country.

A *batey* is a community of impoverished people who live in rudimentary structured housing without running water, electricity, or bathrooms—call it a slum, ghetto, 'hood, it's all the same thing: poverty. There are too many communities like this in the Dominican Republic and our diplomatic missions are typically involved with them in some way or another. *Batey Libertad* is a community supported by Gerald's Yale student association; a Peace Corps volunteer and representatives from USAID and the U.S. Department of Agriculture also served there. They were all doing projects in the vicinity. Gerald talked about his work there practically every time we were together and always encouraged me to visit.

Batey Libertad is located in Esperanza in the northwestern part of the Dominican Republic about a three-hour drive from Santo Domingo. In September 2015, I finally coordinated with Gerald to visit the *batey*. I needed to be back in Santo Domingo by late afternoon because we were scheduled to attend Korean National Day that evening. I left Santo Domingo early that morning and headed north for Esperanza. I arrived before noon and met Gerald and some of his colleagues who also volunteered in the *batey*. They briefed me on what I would experience, and then we drove to the community on the edge of town, nestled between a highway and a large commercial agricultural farm.

People who live in *bateyes* typically work in the agricultural sector in very harsh conditions and receive very little compensation.

Once we were briefed, we all loaded into a small van that was originally built to accommodate about half the size of our group and met with the director at the small *batey* school that the Yale student association funded. Gerald wouldn't let me take my own car and had my driver stay at the volunteer's residence in Esperanza. At first, my driver wasn't pleased about me venturing off without him, but Gerald assured him I would be perfectly safe where we were going.

The school was a two-room cinder block building with small windows near the roof line for ventilation. There was no electricity, and all the desks, books, and supplies were donated and procured by the volunteers. In the Dominican Republic, few students go to school for an entire day. Students generally attend only in the morning or only in the afternoon because when they're old enough, they leave to work with their parents in the fields or to watch the younger children.

This particular school in the *batey* provided a place for the students to study after their half day of school or get further help from the volunteers similar to a tutoring center. It also provided a place where the younger kids who were not old enough to work with their parents could be supervised until their parents got home. Despite the rudimentary facilities, the operation was well-organized and impressive.

I was able to meet many of the students and talk with the director and teachers. Then Gerald took me on a tour of the community. It was small enough to walk through in a short time, and in reality, there weren't really any streets to navigate with a car. As we walked around, it was apparent that Gerald knew every person who lived there. All the kids readily greeted him, and everyone invited us into their homes. At first, I think Gerald had harbored reservations about my seeing where these people slept, but I assured him I was familiar with poverty, and my life was not all champagne and caviar as some people may have assumed.

Gerald also showed me the house where he first lived with a family when he came to the *batey* to volunteer. Although these houses were small and in many cases accommodated four to 10 people with many sleeping in the same room, I was impressed at how clean most of them were kept.

In the middle of the *batey* was a small coffee house that the Yale student group had helped to launch. It was basically the town hall where members of the community would meet for conversation after work and would occasionally spend some of their meager savings to purchase a coffee. They didn't have other options, since no one was going to spend scarce money on an item like soda or beer when they needed every single penny possible to eat.

After a short visit to the coffee shop, we visited the largest house in the *batey* where a man who, for all practical purposes was the mayor, lived. He and his family were sitting on the front steps and could not have been more gracious. It was easy to read his concern for his community and the people who lived there. He and Gerald had a short conversation in Spanish, then we bid him farewell and moved on to a project that the students had built a few years earlier.

The project was a latrine consisting of two bathrooms, a shower area, and a water well. No one in the community had a proper bathroom in their home; the only place to bathe was in the community shower, but it was better than the river that ran behind the *batey* where, prior to these facilities, people would dump trash, relieve themselves, and collect water that had to be boiled for cooking. This all may sound outrageous to an American, but in the Dominican Republic this was rather ordinary. The pollution in these communities is extreme, but they are rarely left a choice. There was no infrastructure for trash collection or disposal, and prior to the latrines, there was no place for human waste.

Why was it important for me to visit *Batey Libertad*? Two reasons: one, my friend Gerald worked hard to provide a better life for the people living there, and two, there was a Peace Corps volunteer living there, and it gave me an opportunity to report back to the embassy the impact the Peace Corps was having in the area.

Many people in the United States believe we should take care of our own and not spend money on foreign lands for these types of initiatives. But taking care of our own also includes developing stable democracies around the world by extending our hand in friendship and providing resources that will make others' lives better. I can assure you if we don't make an effort to provide humanitarian assistance, our adversaries will be more than happy to rush in and do this work for the purpose of political influence and economic gain. The last thing the United States needs is countries like Russia and China influencing our neighbors in the Western Hemisphere to turn against the U.S. I can assure you that when we allow this to happen, it certainly isn't "taking care of our own." If that isn't reason enough for you, then open a Bible and realize our reason for being here in the first place is to extend a hand to those less fortunate.

Breakfast for Equality

As summer 2015 came around, I had been working diligently engaging straight allies who were more than willing to support the equality of LGBT people in the Dominican Republic. I appeared on radio and wrote a few articles published in *Hoy*, the nation's leading newspaper. My social relationships were solid, and I had earned the trust of a large portion of the community of Santo Domingo and Santiago. It was time to for a call to action. I organized the first and probably the only "Breakfast for Equality" at our home. An invitation to the ambassador's residence was always an honor, but this time I was asking people to attend an event supporting the equality of LGBT Dominicans, a first for the country.

It was June 2015, Gay Pride Month, and I had invited the Honorable Randy Berry to be the keynote speaker for the breakfast. Randy was serving as the special envoy for the Human Rights of LGBTI Persons at the State Department in Washington, DC. In addition, Deena Fidas of the Human Rights Campaign was a guest speaker, along with Minou Mirabal, a *diputado* in the Dominican Republic legislature. Minou's mother and two of her aunts were murdered by the dictator Rafael Trujillo for supporting activities to develop a democratic government in the Dominican Republic. Our guests of honor were Dennis and Judy Shepard, whose son, Matthew Shepard, was murdered simply for being gay.

We had met several gay couples from very notable families in Santo Domingo by this time. It was no secret these men were gay, and it was no secret they were couples, but it was never discussed, and they took measures to ensure they were not the subject of conversation in the society class. I asked each of these couples personally if they would host a table at my breakfast. I wanted them to invite their straight friends and family members who supported their relationships. All were willing to do so and a few of them asked others to do the same.

I also reached out to some of my most avid supporters on social media and made the same request. My goal was to have 100 guests at the breakfast, including our table hosts. I was pleasantly surprised that not only did we achieve this goal, but that many straight allies from the embassy community wanted to attend, so they volunteered to serve as ushers and organizers. We held the event with standing room only with more than 100 people attending. It was a beautiful morning all around. I am indebted to Andres Lugo and his company for providing direction and guidance on proper table settings.

Members of the media were invited, and their presence was made known to everyone who had RSVP'd for the event so there were no surprises. In addition to Minou, there was another *diputado* from the Dominican legislature attending in support of his brother. He discussed his support for his brother openly with the press following the event. The media coverage was extremely positive, and nothing derogatory regarding the event was printed in the papers. Photos were published on social media and shared by thousands.

I could not have been more satisfied with the outcome. We raised the Pride flag at the residence and at the embassy, we attended OUTFest—a film festival promoting LGBT subject matter in movies—and we hosted a group of LGBT tourism professionals and met with the minister of tourism on how to help better accommodate LGBT tourists in the Dominican Republic. Most of the Diplomatic community raised the Pride flag at their embassies in solidarity and support along with us. It was uneventful in the press—no real negative reaction, relatively speaking.

Then came the ruling of the Supreme Court of the United States legalizing same sex marriage on June 26, 2015. So many of the couples who had helped me organize and support the events throughout Gay Pride Month 2015 had become friends with the ambassador and me. It was nice to be able to gather with them from time to time and discuss challenges within the community. And when I say challenges I don't necessarily mean LGBT challenges. These men were very successful business men and they had many of the same concerns as every other business man in the country as it pertained to trade agreements and policy considerations. But that particular month they had stepped up and put themselves out there with their family and friends in asking them for their support.

The breakfast was a huge success, and I felt compelled to reward my cohosts for their efforts. I had planned in early June 2015, several weeks prior to the Supreme Court ruling, to host a Sunday afternoon barbecue at our home for those who helped me organize the breakfast. It was a very casual event and an opportunity for me to debrief them, collect their thoughts, and encourage them to continue to support efforts for equality in the Dominican Republic. The barbecue was planned for Sunday, June 28, 2015.

Two days prior, the Supreme Court declared that not allowing same sex couples the equal right to marry as an opposite sex couple was a violation of the Constitution of the United States of America and thereby struck down state laws that prohibited same sex couples from legally marrying. Although we were aware that the ruling was under consideration, we had no idea it was going to happen on that Friday. We were euphoric, and the energy and hope inspired by that decision spread throughout the world.

The Dominican Republic was also inspired by the U.S. Supreme Court decision. Although some of the people in the evangelical community obviously didn't receive the news so well, we received many congratulations from private and government communities on the legal recognition of our marriage.

When you live your entire life from birth through childhood, adolescence, teens, young adulthood, and ultimately into adulthood as an individual without equality, you have a tendency to be less-than-optimistic when it comes to laws changing. Although I felt somewhat confident the Supreme Court would rule in favor of same-sex marriage, it would not have surprised me at all if it had not happened. The idea of being optimistic about the outcome was an overreach for me. But it happened, and it happened without much notice, so it came as a huge surprise for those of us living outside the United States, and obviously a well-received one.

That historic evening, we invited our personal friends to join us for a quick celebratory drink at the JW Marriott, and in all fairness, people have lives and plans, but pretty much all of our friends from the Dominican LGBT community showed up. Never again in my lifetime will I experience something so impacting as on that day. This wasn't just any Supreme Court ruling—it was historic and life-changing for millions of people! There has been no other time in my life when I have felt more euphoric than on Friday, June 26, 2015. I finally became equal in the eyes of the law of my own country. I was very excited to lift a glass of champagne with my friends and those who supported equality!

The Deep End of the Pool

The following Sunday we gathered with our close friends at our residence for the pre-planned barbecue and debrief about the Breakfast for Equality. It was a typical day in the Dominican Republic—beautiful, sunny, and in the high 70s. We fired up the grill, cooked hamburgers and hot dogs, continued to talk about the Supreme Court ruling in total disbelief and even speculated whether it could be real or whether somehow the U.S. Congress might attempt a Constitutional amendment outlawing our equality? For the most part, the conversation remained extremely positive and celebratory.

Following lunch and as the afternoon began to heat up, our guests changed into their swimming trunks and enjoyed the sun and a dip in the pool. As the afternoon concluded, I snapped a picture to commemorate our day of celebration. And then without regard or thought, I haphazardly decided to share that photo with my social media friends via Facebook.

It seemed innocent enough. I figured what is wrong with a group of friends gathering at someone's home for a barbecue and afternoon swim? In most cases absolutely nothing, but then this was not most cases. My husband was the U.S. ambassador to the Dominican Republic, and there were people of influence and people in the media who didn't like us—not only didn't like us, but made every effort on a daily basis to be as disparaging and vulgar as possible about us in the media.

By this point I had become numb to the daily bigot briefing, as I had come to call the morning stories in the newspapers. The public affairs team at the embassy gathered stories every morning from the daily periodicals and summarized them into a briefing for the ambassador and the State Department in Washington. There was always a mix of salacious stories from news sources placed in that briefing that really didn't have anything to do with the efforts of the embassy. I later discovered that these types of stories were irrelevant and shouldn't have been included in that briefing. Clearly the person who was including them didn't take the most honorable approach to his or her job. It was obvious that person was doing his or her best to send an undesirable message about the ambassador to Washington. However, the news story that was about to unfold was one of my own making and one in which I clearly should have expressed a greater degree of discretion.

I posted the picture of us in the swimming pool on social media without really thinking about the significance of some of the people in that picture. The next morning, Monday, June 29, 2015, there the picture was, front and center on the title page of one of the morning papers, *Diario Libre*. Although *Diario Libre* was not a legitimate periodical or well respected, the picture of the ambassador and his husband with a group of men in a swimming pool at his residence was fodder enough for the entire country to talk. Dominicans are not unlike Americans: they love gossip as much as anyone else. The issue with the picture wasn't so much the presence of the ambassador and his husband, it was more about who from the Dominican Republic was in the picture. The gossip groups on WhatsApp began to disseminate the news faster than the radio talk show hosts could spread it across the airways.

Personally, I was unaffected by the whole situation. For me, it was just another day and another negative story that I had become numb to long ago. But for my good friends who had worked their entire lives to build businesses and reputations within the social and business community in the Dominican Republic, it was devastating and humiliating for them, and more so for their families. I admit that at first, I was disappointed with my friends for being upset. Looking at it through my American lens, we had done absolutely nothing wrong, and there was nothing inappropriate about that picture. But unfortunately, perception is reality when it comes to the gossip wheel.

When it comes to acceptable social behavior in the Dominican Republic, the rules do not apply equally to all. Opposite sex couples can practically have sex in public and all will just turn a blind eye. The swim attire young women wear to the beach is more revealing than that of an exotic dancer at a gentlemen's club in Las Vegas, and that doesn't remotely compare to the "uniforms" of the cheerleaders/dancers at a Dominican baseball game. Dominican baseball cheerleaders are nothing but professional exotic dancers who leave practically nothing to the imagination, and it all takes place right in front of a family gathering.

To me the idea of a group of men taking a picture in a swimming pool is completely modest at best. My initial reaction when everyone was making such a big deal about the pool picture was, "How dare these hypocrites insinuate we were up to something inappropriate?" I was also a little offended by my friends becoming upset, because I thought they were buying into the whole cultural hypocrisy that was forcing LGBT people to remain in the closet. But I was wrong.

I was being completely insensitive to my friends' position based on my own personal experiences and not taking into consideration their life experiences and how this would impact them socially and professionally. For this I am truly sorry for posting that picture and the humiliation I caused them. They were not living in a house with a big American flag in front surrounded by a large wall and guards. They were not escorted around town in an armored vehicle and didn't have security guards to accompany them to events. They were living, eating, and breathing in a society that judged them every day for being born. They had to live and survive socially and professionally in a culture that placed daily hurdles in front of them, and every day the hurdles would get higher. I was wrong, and I apologize for my insensitivity and the embarrassment I caused them.

Unlike other negative or salacious stories the local papers printed about us, this one was different because what I came to realize is this was not about me or the ambassador. This was about bringing embarrassment on the people who were simply accepting an invitation to spend the day at our home. *Diario Libre* intentionally set out to harm a group of people by damaging their reputations in the hope it could somehow inflict a negative image on those who accepted invitations to the ambassador's private residence. As well, the story clearly set out to damage the reputation of the U.S. embassy and disseminated blatantly false information. The intent was to inflict shame and embarrassment on all who had been present.

We obviously demanded a retraction to no avail. After much consideration and discussion with my husband I made the decision to no longer allow *Diario Libre* or its reporters or representatives access to private events at our home. This was communicated to our public affairs team and was met with some resistance by certain members, but I was not backing down. I may not have had many liberties within the embassy community but one liberty I did have was who was and was not permitted in my home. And as long as I was a resident in that house, *Diario Libre* would not set foot on the grounds.

I must go on record here to inform you I reached out to *Diario Libre* through my personal resources in the media community to no avail. I was more than willing to have a discussion with the owner of the paper in an attempt to express the truth about that day, and I hoped he could see fit to at least soften the harshness displayed in his paper, but I never received a response.

There were other online news outlets that took that story and printed stock photos of a more damaging impression indicating we had hosted male sex workers and had engaged in a sex party. The entire thing was completely outrageous and *Diario Libre* refused to set the record straight, so I felt completely justified in banning them from my home. The story died relatively quickly, and some other ridiculous story took its place. Unfortunately, my attempts at improving the relationship with *Diario Libre* never proved fruitful. *Diario Libre* continued to cover all embassy events, just not private events at our residence.

Un-Invited

A few weeks after the barbecue, we hosted a private event at the residence with our good friends David Ortiz and Nelson Cruz for an MLB educational initiative in cooperation with USAID. Because the event was taking place at our home, we invited selected members of the media based on their readership to help promote the cause to the community it most benefited. The Dominican Republic has a very large media community and it is impossible to host all of them for every event with rare exceptions like our Fourth of July celebration.

I had indicated to the public affairs team very clearly that *Diario Libre* was no longer allowed at my home and under no circumstances should be extended an invitation for the MLB event. When the media arrived that evening to set up for the event, *Diario Libre* showed up. According to sources, they had sent their reporters to our residence for the event because a member of our public affairs team invited them, only to be told by our public affairs representative that the ambassador had specifically expressed they were not allowed to enter and cover the event.

There are a couple of wrongs here that need to be corrected. That decision to not include *Diario Libre* was not made by the ambassador. It was made by me and was supported by the ambassador. *Diario Libre* should have never known about the event in the first place or received an invitation to attend. I could never prove my suspicion, but clearly they were somehow informed the event was taking place and then were purposely turned away, so as to reflect negatively on the ambassador. I have no doubt this situation was manufactured by a member of our embassy public affairs team who wanted to send more negative information to the State Department in Washington. No doubt there were enemies in our own embassy. It was difficult enough working in a country where there were people of influence who did everything possible to work against our success, but having to navigate the bureaucracy of fellow colleagues' ill intentions made it even more challenging.

Fortunately, this story also died a quick death, and *Diario Libre*'s attempt to cast a second net with the story of their being turned away from a private event at our residence only made them look more foolish and solidified their reputation in the media community as one that perpetuated fake news. We continued our work, heads up and eyes forward.

11: Going Home

Our return to the United States began on election night, November 8, 2016, a few months before we actually departed the Dominican Republic. It is traditional that all U.S. embassies around the world host an event celebrating the election of a U.S. president. "Democracy in Action" we like to call it, showcasing to our host countries how elections work in a democracy. Career State Department diplomats are "non-partisan" when serving abroad, they don't publicly participate in campaigns happening back home and having political conversations with fellow colleagues is taboo. So the idea behind hosting an event for local society to celebrate our election and show the host country how we come together and support our newly elected government despite what side of the aisle you are on or what candidate you support seems reasonable.

But the U.S. presidential election of 2016 was not reasonable. Hell, it wasn't even civil. The campaign between Donald Trump and Hillary Clinton was beyond embarrassing on the global stage. All level of decorum was tossed out the window and the name calling, bullying, and labeling by candidate Trump reduced him to the image of a third-grade school yard bully. I have been known to throw a slur or two in my day—I am not pretending to be standing on some moral high ground here—but I am not running a campaign for president of the United States, and most importantly, I have never intentionally tried to inflict harm on the United States. I have visited more than 50 countries in my lifetime and I am always keenly aware when I am on foreign soil that whatever impression I leave through my interactions with locals is their impression of America. Donald Trump embarrassed the United States with his campaign antics and continues to do so to this day.

Election night was the beginning of the end of our tenure in the Dominican Republic. I had a conversation with my husband in early October 2016 where I predicted that Hillary Clinton was going to lose the election. It was all anyone could talk about and although I refrained from any discussions with locals—despite being asked upwards of 30 times a day, "Is Hillary going to win?"—I would always respond that "the American people will get it right." That same month, I had 21 events of my own on the calendar—one wedding in Las Vegas, four house guests scattered throughout the month, and a principal visit from Dr. Jill Biden, the second lady of the United States. These were scheduled events in addition to the routine lunches, dinners, and cocktail receptions we typically attended regularly. It may sound like a chaotic schedule but actually, that was a pretty normal life for me during our tenure in the Dominican Republic. I only point this out to indicate how impossible it was not to be asked about the U.S. election. We were faced with it at every corner. I was dreading the election, I was not looking forward to hosting a huge event with Dominican society and government dignitaries while pretending to be happy should my intuition about the outcome come to fruition.

A few days before the election, Raul Baz Suarez asked me to appear as an election results analyst/co-host for his segment about the U.S. election on live television. I jumped at the chance; I really didn't want to be at the embassy election party. We all have our talents and pretending is not one of mine. I relished in the opportunity to discuss the election as it was unfolding. We had set some ground rules about asking me personal questions on the air, but other than that, it was really about describing to the Dominican television audience how the electoral college was calculated and the significance of winning states like Florida. It was a short segment, but it got me out of the event for a few hours because the television studio was on the other side of town. By the time I returned to the embassy election event, it was clear that Donald Trump was going to win. The writing was on the wall and every major network was clearly leaning toward a Trump victory.

The remainder of the evening was a bit of a blur and I didn't leave our home for a few days after the election. I was through discussing the election and I certainly wanted no part of a conversation about the outcome. But eventually life moves on.

Saying Goodbye to the Dominican Republic

In the days following the election of Donald Trump, I felt like I had been punched in the stomach and was unable to catch my breath. It all sounds so dramatic, but I honestly think I could have dealt with Mitt Romney being elected president over Donald Trump. Mitt Romney might have been extremely conservative and definitely did not believe in the equality of the gay community, but at least he was a seasoned government servant and although we probably don't agree on a single policy, I believe him to be a decent human being.

A few weeks passed and Wally was preparing for his ambassador's speech at the annual Thanksgiving Lunch at the American Chamber of Commerce in Santo Domingo. It was tradition for the U.S. ambassador to host the Thanksgiving lunch, as Thanksgiving is an American holiday. This would be the first major public appearance for Wally following the election and it was also one where the media would be present and asking a million questions about the U.S. election of Donald Trump.

We discussed the approach he should take; clearly he would have to mention the election, the state of democracy, and the traditions of the American people. It would need to be eloquent and contain all the intricacies of diplomacy. The narrative was important for another reason: it would also be Wally's resignation speech. We kept that part confidential between just us; we knew if embassy personnel got their hands on the resignation portion of the speech, it would be leaked to the media and it was imperative we controlled the narrative. First and foremost, Wally was nominated by President Obama to serve as his eyes and ears in the Dominican Republic as a member of his administration, so the idea of continuing to serve another president was not something Wally ever entertained. Second, there was no way Wally was going to work for Donald Trump. Their values were not compatible. And finally, he was not going to hear the words "You're Fired" from Donald Trump, so a resignation was the appropriate action to take. At the end of his speech, Wally resigned as the U.S. ambassador to the Dominican Republic effective January 20, 2017.

Some people are so predictable when it comes to lack of consideration for other human beings. It was December 23, 2016, when all the ambassadors that were "politically appointed" by President Obama received a notification that as of January 20, 2017, they would no longer be employed by the State Department and were asked to vacate their positions and the CMRs where they lived by 12:00 noon that day. The letter stated there would be "no exceptions." Typically there is consideration given to ambassadors with extenuating circumstances, including those with children in school, to extend their appointments until a replacement can be found. One ambassador's wife was going through chemotherapy treatments, but Donald Trump and his transition team refused to allow an extension until those treatments could be completed. Our close friends had to rent a home in a foreign country until their children could complete their current semester at school before returning to the United States. These were unnecessary and avoidable hardships. So much for a happy holiday.

There are some things the State Department accomplishes extremely well and one of those is moving people! I can't speak for other career diplomats, but when the foreign service moves an ambassador, it is done very well. They had the most professional packers who were extremely efficient. Our personal belongings were packed and shipped to and from the Dominican Republic without one single thing missing or broken.

There was one hiccup on our return that happened with our personal vehicle, but it wasn't the State Department's fault. It was shipped to Miami and then the State Department contracted with a transportation company to take it to Texas. Somewhere in the panhandle of Florida in the early morning hours, the truck carrying our car to Texas was involved in a severe accident due to extreme fog. The car didn't suffer a lot of physical damage but sadly there was a fatality in the accident, so our car was impounded for several weeks. When the car finally arrived in Texas, some type of oil-like substance had destroyed the paint. All was repaired and insurance covered the cost, but we had to be without a car for a few months longer than we had planned.

Wheels Up

January 20, 2017—Inauguration Day, or in our case Departure Day—arrived. All our personal belongs except a few suitcases and our dogs Clinton and Carter had been packed in mid-December and shipped to Dallas. Wally and I decided to return to our "home" after living in the Dominican Republic. Texas was home because that was where we first met, where we bought our first home, and of course, where Wally was from. We still owned our home but it was leased and we couldn't move back into it immediately. Just like I remember the first time we drove through the gates of the residence on November 26, 2013, I remember the last time we drove out. Many of the same people who greeted us that first day at the airport when we arrived in-country were with us when we left on our last day.

I was sad, but not because I was leaving or going to miss all the wonderful people I had befriended. I could always go back to the Dominican Republic and visit them, after all I had been traveling there for most of my adult life. I was sad because I didn't know what was going to happen in my own country. I wasn't comfortable about what we were returning to. When we arrived at the airport, our entire team went to a private lounge where we could have some time to reminisce and say goodbye. We all hugged, and of course there were a few tears but more than anything, there was so much love in that room.

The security detail that provided my husband's around-the-clock protection was there along with my dear friend Grissette Vasquez, just like the day we arrived. Our team was there to hold our hand as we departed the last time as diplomats. Nelson Ramirez was Wally's head bodyguard and directed and coordinated all of his security. As we boarded the plane he walked us down the jet bridge and shook our hands for the last time, doing his job and ensuring we were safely on our flight. I always sit at the window and Wally always sits on the aisle, as we rolled down the runway for the last time courtesy of the U.S. State Department I looked out the window and there was our entire team and security detail waiting on the tarmac for us to takeoff. The ambassador's security never leaves the airport until your plane is in the air and even though the ambassadorship had officially come to an end, the security detail waited for wheels up.

The flight home to Texas was as rough as the flight to the Dominican Republic had been. It wasn't the fault of anyone specific or even the airline—it was Clinton and Carter, our dogs. From the moment we took off from Santo Domingo until we landed in Miami, they whined and barked loudly during the entire flight. Nothing would calm them down. By the time we got to Miami, Wally wanted to rent a car and drive the rest of the way. Finally, we made it to Texas, where it all had started 25 years before. Home.

The Difference a Day Makes

The experience of serving the American people and the United States of America is something that is unique for those who have the opportunity. It's not a job, it's a commitment to doing everything possible to ensure that we pave a path for a better future for all people. U.S. soldiers fight wars and lose their lives for democracy, politicians sacrifice spending time with their kids to protect our freedom, government employees work for far less pay than they could make in the private sector to lend their talents so our government can function at the highest levels. These are commitments at various levels, but commitments nonetheless.

Wally and I were so privileged to have played a small part in representing the United States in a foreign land and I am very proud of the work we accomplished there. The experience was not without its critics, but one thing I have learned in life is that no matter who you are or what you do or how good you do it, someone will have an opinion. I certainly express mine, after all it is our First Amendment right as Americans.

Returning to the private sector after such an experience is not an easy process. We landed in Dallas, and Donald Trump had been sworn in as the president of the United States. Our dear friend Kim Merrill picked us up at the DFW airport and was kind enough to take us to her home for a few days until we could get sorted with moving into the house we rented during our transition. We curled up in bed with Clinton and Carter and went to sleep.

The next morning everything had changed. We didn't have a home to call our own, we didn't have jobs, we didn't have a car, and we had to rely on the kindness of our friends for basically everything. Life was beautiful but what a difference a day makes.

12: Conclusion: Working to Improve Democracy

I realized my passion for politics and democracy when I was young. Before meeting Governor Boren on that fall day in 1978, my only impressions of politicians were they seemed to lie and get in trouble a lot. In some cases things haven't changed all that much since then. I was only 10 years old when Nixon resigned from office. Obviously, I was too young to understand what was happening or why it happened but I was old enough to understand that it must have been important because that was all the adults around me were talking about. I also remember him being called a Republican. I didn't know what a Republican was but I thought it must have been bad because Nixon got in a lot of trouble and had to stop being president.

I share this bit of history about my political experience because it is important for us understand that young people are influenced in so many ways—not only by the adults around them but by experiences they have, curriculums they are exposed to, and the news they see on television and the internet. Despite my initial impressions and my lifetime of experience in the political arena, I still faithfully believe in democracy and the rule of law. It is unfortunate that political ideology is now defined simply by labels. Party platforms were designed to promote policy and to encourage legislation that benefits all affected, not for the benefit of creating power and control over those who are on the other side.

I believe in the purity of our political system, and until recently, that people of both political parties serve the public or are elected to public office to make the world a better place for future generations. I have met many elected officials who are good people and I have met a few who were good people who lost their way. With the exception of Donald Trump, I do not know of anyone who initially ran for public office whose goal was truly self-serving.

The election of Donald Trump confirms now more than ever the necessity for good, honest, and genuine people to serve the greater good for the American people. The polarization of our American culture and the development of identity politics are deteriorating our democracy.

Our system of checks and balances is being questioned. Our journalists are being attacked at every turn and without them, the transparency of our democracy fades. Our elections are being manipulated by domestic and foreign influencers alike. The state of affairs within our democratic process is driving our young, educated generation further and further from the political arena. This is extraordinarily dangerous for future generations because their future is being guided without their influence. We must not labor the future generations with the division of our past. In a democracy, unity or the effort to pursue unity is paramount, for division will eventually kill a democracy as it divides against itself.

I hear from my peers as well as those older than me that the next generation should listen, learn, and wait their turn—they don't have the life experience to participate in such a complicated undertaking. I disagree. There are plenty of people my age and older who are supposed to have used their life experience and wisdom to guide the future of America, yet they have really messed things up for the next generation. I'm not saying that all young people should seek political careers. But it certainly doesn't mean that just because you are old you have the wisdom and experience to guide the future of our country. Good, honest, and genuine people come in all ages. Those who care about the lives of future generations and the stability of our democracy should exercise their right to influence our government for the greater good of all people. Being good, honest, and genuine has nothing to do with being perfect—we are way past the burden of attempting to elect perfection to public office. After all, we elected Donald Trump.

No one is perfect anyway. Our imperfections shouldn't be barrier to our participation in democracy. However, serving your own self-interests and personally benefitting from the power of being in office should be a barrier. This is how dictators are born—combined with the lack of participation by a country's citizens.

Our democratic system of electing representatives is deteriorating in the United States. Elected and appointed political leaders are failing their constituencies by only representing the interest of the majority. Once elected to office, a representative should not set aside the needs and concerns of the minority who may have supported their opponent. By doing so they are dismissing the opportunity to engage in a dialogue with their constituency that has an alternative view of progress. They are also disregarding an opportunity to engage with and develop a relationship that can ultimately bring about cohesion within their communities. Just because you supported the winner in an election doesn't give you and your views priority in influencing policy and just because you supported the loser in an election doesn't mean you no longer have the right to have your voice heard.

The beautiful thing about democracy is it doesn't take a Mensa IQ to participate. Democracy was designed to allow all citizens a seat at the table and to have their voice heard, either by voting for or questioning the representative who speaks for them. If our democracy is failing us all on many fronts, then we are failing our democracy. It is our right to vote and express our ideas and concerns about our future, just as it is our right to stay at home and do nothing. Either way, though, we are accountable for our actions or inactions.

Approximately 36 percent of the world's counties do not hold free and fair elections. In my global travels, I have seen governments that isolate their citizens and restrict their exposure to outside influence and education. This type of governmental control ultimately fails. Attempting to restrict and isolate people from education and experiences results in economic hardship and poverty. United States citizens, however, are born with the inalienable right to "life, liberty, and the pursuit of happiness." This birthright privilege can never be revoked by an outside force and my concern is if we choose not to exercise our right to vote, that one day an "inside" force will attempt to revoke that right. Who'll be accountable then?

Not every young person will have the experience of meeting the governor of a state and be influenced in a positive way like I was. I was influenced when Governor Boren won his election to be the U.S. senator from Oklahoma and he influenced me throughout his career. He was an outstanding politician and good man who served the best interest of his entire constituency, not just those who supported him. I believe he was an excellent example of what a good, honest, and genuine politician who represents all people to the best of his ability should look like.

Donald Trump's slogan "America First"—the belief that Americans sacrifice our own opportunities when we extend our influence in developing global democracy—could not be further from the truth. It is ultimately in the best interest of America to promote democracy, education, leadership, public health, infrastructure, and so many other elements of foreign policy around the globe. Americans benefit from global trade and strong foreign economies. Foreign policy is not a zero sum game; we cannot prosper in a world of us versus them, because without cooperation on a global scale, there is no winner. We must look at the 192 countries in the world as 192 opportunities to where we can sell our goods and services and form diplomatic relationships that support our point of view when we face adversarial hurdles. Creating commerce globally is far better for the future generations of the world than creating division, isolation, and war.

Despite our differences on policy, taxation, religion, and other divisive subjects, we as Americans can always find some basic commonality as long as we agree on the basic premise that "all humans are created equal." The question I often ask myself is where do we, as the human race, go from here? I would love to have that answer. I've found that we move forward better collectively with cooperation than alone with antagonism. "Forward" was President Obama's campaign slogan and it meant forward for everyone, not just those who supported him. President Obama inspired a vision and motivated so many globally. As human beings, we are truly capable of accomplishing anything we could think of—and that is how my husband became a U.S. ambassador.

I still travel the world working with marginalized populations and organizations that promote the equality of all people. In emerging economies and developing democracies it is always the minority populations that get left behind, and without their participation in their own governments their voices will never be heard. The challenge minority populations face results from all sorts of hurdles including lack of education, money, infrastructure, gender-based persecution, religious persecution, and cultural and sexual identity. It takes a lot more effort to beat people down than to extend them an opportunity to improve their lives. That is what democracy is designed for, to improve the lives of its citizens, all of its citizens.

My experiences from traveling the world and living in a foreign country taught me so much more about life than anything I ever learned in a book. That is not to say education is not important or should be cast aside, but just like any of our experiences, we benefit far greater from them when our exposure is broadened. I am no expert on education policy but I am confident that if the U.S. public education system provided a path for all students to experience a year or even a semester abroad, we would have a more unified and global-minded world. I have seen and heard people get angry in public spaces because people are having a conversation in a language other than English. I can't comprehend that close-minded approach to patriotism. I once worked with a guy who spoke seven languages fluently and watched as he had the ability to seamlessly engage with a variety of people and enrich his travel experiences without the need to depend on others to read a menu. The fact is we don't need to all speak multiple languages fluently, but we all need to respect others' chosen language of communication. I can promise you that simple gesture will ensure your experience will be far more meaningful and pleasant.

It is my hope that we, the United States, will continue to provide guidance and pathways toward global democracy. That doesn't mean that every country should have a system of government that mirrors the United States. Democracy takes on many definitions and accommodates many styles of government structure, but the one commonality is it provides its people freedom of choice in their personal lives and provides a structure where we all can have an opportunity to grow and prosper. This life is nothing but possibility and opportunity, and there is always a door in front of us. The only action required is to reach forward and turn the handle.

Afterword

When we returned to the United States after our tenure in the Dominican Republic, I found myself at yet another crossroad in life. I love the options a crossroad puts in front of me. As tempting as it would be to turn around and go back, life doesn't allow us do-overs. Choosing the safe path might provide you an easy way, but not one that will challenge you to grow. The challenging path forward is always the most rewarding. I have always found when I overreach on that challenging path, there is always someone along the way who is willing to extend a hand of support.

I decided to pursue another level of education and applied for a graduate program at the University of Oxford. I needed references in order for my application to be considered for acceptance, and I found former colleagues who were willing to speak out for me. I needed emotional encouragement and found many friends and family who continuously reaffirmed I was worthy. And during my time at Oxford I found my fellow students more than willing to share information and spend endless hours explaining platforms and theories to me. By choosing a path forward I found plenty of friends, family, colleagues, and perfect strangers who extended that helping hand.

I have faced many hurdles in life, many I wish I had never had to face, but despite them, I have had more than my fair share of blessings. Despite my fantastic ability to annoy those I love, especially my husband, I hope somewhere one day my spirit will reflect positively on the world. Blessings result in an obligation to extend your hand to those who walk the path behind you and ensure their opportunity for success exceeds yours. That is why we are all here in the first place. Some of you have no idea where to go from here. Me too, but I challenge you: whatever motivation you have as of a result of your life experience and your moments, share that motivation so those who follow can reap your blessings. That is how you succeed!

In the Dominican Republic, I was able to achieve certain successes under the radar because of my own personal experiences. I know what it is like to be looked down on, discarded, and ridiculed just because you are poor. I know what it is like for people to assume all sorts of outrageous things about me because I am gay. I have experienced all levels of discrimination as a result of my economic position, sexual orientation, and cultural and native identity. I have always been in the minority. Visiting impoverished neighborhoods didn't scare me because I had grown up like that and learned not to be scared of people just because they had no money. So, in some ways I look back on my crappy childhood only to realize it is as much of who I am today as any other experience I have had in my lifetime. It clearly had a motivating influence on the person I am today.

If this means I am a bleeding-heart liberal, then I wear that title as a badge of honor. While I'm no Robin Hood, I am a man of Christ, and the Lord Jesus teaches us to extend our hand to all those in need, not just those we pick and choose. I advocate separation of church and state, but what I don't understand is how one can advocate for a Christian nation yet destroy government programs that help stabilize the lives of those less fortunate.

Where does life go from here? I have no idea. I am once again at a crossroad and I can assure but one thing, it is time for a new adventure. I will always be involved in the political arena. I feel an obligation as a citizen to participate and ensure my voice is heard, and also to provide an influence for those who can't speak for themselves. I may or may not influence the position of my elected representative but at a minimum I know it wasn't for a lack of effort. We live in a global society full of rules, regulations, and policies that affect us on every level of life. Those of us in the United States and other democracies have an opportunity to temper those positions to ensure they are improving our opportunities, not restricting our abilities. Encourage and embrace change for we cannot improve our future without change. We can always make things better for everyone and improving life for some does not have to be at the expense of others.

We must and can do better in the United States, and at the same time we can extend our hands of diplomacy to those countries that struggle in their quest for freedom and liberty and justice. The bottom line: life is not about you, it's about what you do with life. It's about making the world a better place for someone else and extending a hand to others when you have been blessed.

Acknowledgments

To Ambassador James W. Brewster, the smartest, most genuine, sincere, amazing, caring, loving, generous, and giving human being I have ever known: I am thankful for your patience and for supporting me to tell my story through my experiences. I love you!

I have always fancied myself as a writer. I have written blogs and editorials and even had a few published, but when I tackled the initiative of writing a book, my talents were stretched. I am a firm believer we never do anything alone—and I certainly didn't achieve this accomplishment by myself—therefore I want to acknowledge those who stood by me along the way.

For the hundreds of you who listened to me over the years pour my heart out over a few drinks and encouraged me to keep moving this process forward, thank you! To all of my friends and family who continually visited my husband and me in the Dominican Republic during our tenure and provided words of encouragement and support, thank you!

I would like to specifically acknowledge my dear friend Pat Croke—without your years of guidance and support none of these experiences would have ever happened for me. I thank Sue for always having a positive word to share. Tommy, Heather, John, Adam, and Mary Ellen, who are my brothers and sisters from another mother, and I love you so much.

Moises and Austria, I don't have the words to express my love for you and your family, those words will forever live in my heart and I share my heart with you.

Maribel, Donel, Antonio, Montse, Joselito, Arecelis, Aramis, Judy, Paola, and Omar, I am blessed to have had your support and friendship all these years. Tomas and Yahaira, thank you for all those times you helped me escape the pressure and for sharing your friendship with me. Carlos, Andres, Jose, Jesus, Ben, Gerald, Carlos Emil, Brock, Gary, Luis, Ken, and Jeremy, you will always be my posse.

Cristela, Kiko, and Belky, you will forever be my family and thank you for your dedication and caring for me. I miss you. Paola, no human could have ever endured me as long as you have. Thank you for sticking with me.

Rafa and Amado, may life bless you and your families as much as you have blessed me.

My dear Grissette, I never would have survived without you and I am beyond thankful for the support, encouragement, and guidance you gave me without expectation.

Nelson and your team, thank you for taking care of my husband and protecting him. Carlos, thank you for your dedication and protecting me.

Tommy for believing in me and helping me manage our business until I grew up. Eric and Craig, for jumping off the cliff and knowing we could really accomplish equality and help elect a president!

Jimmie and Dessie (my mom and dad), despite all the hardships we endured throughout our lives, we are blessed and I am thankful for your love.

Shannon, you were the first person who read this mess before editing and encouraged me to continue down the path. You have no idea how much gratitude I feel for your support.

Anne and Phyllis, thank you! My words would be nothing more than thoughts scattered on a page without you.

About the Author

Bob J. Satawake is living the quintessential rags-to-(sort of)-riches American dream, rising from modest beginnings in rural Oklahoma to serving as senior policy advisor to Ambassador James "Wally" Brewster in the Dominican Republic—and beyond. Bob's passion for championing human rights is the backbone for the projects he advocates. While in Santo Domingo, he chaired various human rights committees at the U.S. embassy, and effected positive change in pursuing justice for victims of gender-based violence and human/sex trafficking in the Dominican Republic. Bob fights for equality and served as senior advisor to three USAID LGBT projects while in the Dominican Republic.

As a former diplomat, Bob maintains relationships at the highest levels of government and the private sector, focusing on foreign policy relationships that forward the stability of emerging democracies. Bob is an advisor to the National Democratic Institute (NDI) and focuses on minority and LGBTI inclusion in developing democracies throughout the world as chair of the Equal Voices Advisory Council. With NDI, Bob has traveled the world partaking in diplomatic missions that promote democracy, human rights, diversity, inclusion, and foreign policy in Georgia, Ukraine, Colombia, Serbia, and Guatemala.

While owner and managing partner of the Chicago Luxury Group, Bob pursued various philanthropic and other social and political activities. He served on the board for BUILD, a Chicago nonprofit aimed at reducing gang activity for at-risk inner city students. Bob also served as a member of the National Board of Directors for Victory Fund, a nonprofit bi-partisan organization that provides educational and leadership training for LGBT candidates running for elected office.

Bob is a writer, speaker, lecturer, blogger, and contributor to various news publications regarding humanitarian rights and marginalized people. He has spoken before international institutions, universities, nonprofits, and other outlets regarding corporate social responsibility and promoting human rights. Bob recently completed his graduate diploma in global business–masters level at the University of Oxford

Said School of Business and is always looking for the next opportunity to leave the world better than he found it.